UNDERSTANDING MISUNDERSTANDINGS

A PRACTICAL GUIDE

TO MORE

SUCCESSFUL

HUMAN

INTERACTION

ROBERT L. YOUNG

UNDERSTANDING

MISUNDERSTANDINGS

UNIVERSITY OF TEXAS PRESS, AUSTIN

The Self-Monitoring Scale on pages 63–64 is reproduced courtesy of Mark Snyder. It originally appeared in the article "Self-Monitoring of Expressive Behavior" in *Journal of Personality and Social Psychology* 30: 526–537.

Copyright © 1999 by the University of Texas Press
All rights reserved
Printed in the United States of America

First edition, 1999

Requests for permission to reproduce material from this work should be sent to Permissions, University of Texas Press, Box 7819, Austin, TX 78713-7819.

♾ The paper used in this book meets the minimum requirements of ANSI/NISO Z39.48-1992 (R1997) (Permanence of Paper).

LIBRARY OF CONGRESS CATALOGING-IN-PUBLICATION DATA

Young, Robert L. (Robert Louis), 1949–
    Understanding misunderstandings : a practical guide to more successful human interaction / Robert L. Young. — 1st ed.
        p.   cm.
    Includes bibliographical references and index.
    ISBN 0-292-79605-6 (alk. paper). — ISBN 0-292-79606-4 (pbk. : alk. paper)
        1. Miscommunication.   2. Interpersonal communication.   I. Title.
BF637.C45Y69   1999
153.6—dc21   99-13582

To Louis

and Louise;

for Katie

and Nick

CONTENTS

PREFACE

All social interaction is based on the assumption that whatever we say or do will be understood more or less as it was intended. It is clear, however, that the course of social interaction is often determined by misspeaks, mishearings, misinterpretations, and other forms of misunderstanding. When we misunderstand each other, we are likely to respond in inappropriate, unproductive, and sometimes destructive ways. Misunderstandings can produce frustration, embarrassment, shame, and misdirected anger, which can disrupt social interaction and sometimes damage interpersonal relationships. Understanding exactly how and why interpersonal misunderstandings come about can help us avoid them and more effectively handle them when they do occur.

Inasmuch as misunderstandings create practical problems, a book about them would seem to benefit from a practical approach. As an academic sociologist I am convinced that there is nothing more potentially practical than a good theory. Unfortunately, the literature of the social and behavioral sciences is replete with good theories and valuable insights that never find their way into public thinking and policy. Because those of us involved in scientific pursuits communicate with each other through the often esoteric languages of science and philosophy, most of what we produce in scholarly journals never finds its way into public discourse. Moreover, because most of us consider it our job to produce and critique knowledge, rather than apply it, we rarely attempt the difficult yet vital task of translating that knowledge into a language that is meaningful to professionals, community leaders, and other educated members of the public. This book is an attempt to do just that. It represents more than a decade of thinking and writing around and about a topic that I consider central to our ability to function effectively as social beings. The ideas presented here are drawn primarily from the disciplines of sociology, psychology, linguistics, and anthropology, and I hope that they adequately reflect my appreciation for the contributions of scholars from each of those disciplines.

In the interest of making the book appealing and informative to students and educated laypeople, I have sacrificed much of the depth and attention to detail characteristic of more scholarly work. Because of its breadth, however, I hope that even those scholars who find my coverage of the insights provided by their own discipline lacking will nevertheless benefit from exposure to the ideas that other disciplines bring to the topic.

Inasmuch as I have documented the scholarly sources from which I have drawn, those interested in a more thoroughgoing and systematic study of the various topics on which I touch will have a place to start.

Many people deserve thanks for assistance and inspiration along the way. First and foremost, I thank those students, friends, and acquaintances who shared the personal experiences that constitute many of the examples that appear throughout the book. Their stories provided data for my analysis and gave life to my otherwise inadequate prose. In all cases, their names have been changed to preserve their anonymity. I also thank my department and university for the time and resources required to conduct such a project, as well as my colleagues, who helped direct me to sources of information in areas with which they were more familiar than I. Finally, to adequately thank Carol Thompson would require another book. Having suffered through this one, however, she would probably prefer a simple thanks.

UNDERSTANDING MISUNDERSTANDINGS

1 Introduction

Interaction and

Misunderstanding

(Costello) *On the Saint Louis team we have Who's on first, What's on second, I Don't Know's on third.*

(Abbott) *That's what I want to find out. I want you to tell me the names of the fellows on the Saint Louis team.*

(Costello) *I, I'm telling you Who's on first, What's on second, I Don't Know's on third.*

(Abbott) *You know the fellows' names?*

(Costello) *Yes.*

(Abbott) *Well then, Who's playing first?*

(Costello) *Yes.*

(Abbott) *I mean, the fellow's name on first base.*

(Costello) *Who.*

(Abbott) *The fellow playing first base for Saint Louis.*

(Costello) *Who.*

(Abbott) *The guy on first base.*

(Costello) *Who is on first.*

(Abbott) *Well, what are you asking me for?*

(Costello) *I'm not asking you, I'm telling you, Who is on first.*

(Abbott) *I'm asking you: Who's on first?*

UNIVERSAL PICTURES *(1945)*

Do you know anyone you just can't seem to communicate with, no matter how hard you try? If you make a joke, they take it seriously. If you pay them a compliment, they assume you have a hidden agenda. If you make a suggestion, they take it as an order. Such encounters are frustrating, and the results are usually not comedic. Whether such people are co-workers, acquaintances, or relatives, it seems that most of what you do or say passes through some sort of distortion filter before it registers on their brain, and it may not work any better as you try to make sense of their actions. In fact, it seems that one or both of you are in a perpetual state of confusion over just what has gone wrong, and you find yourself describing one after another of your interactions as a misunderstanding. It would be frustrating enough if such experiences were restricted to a few problem individuals we might be able to avoid much of the time. Unfortunately, we also experience such difficulties with people we know intimately and feel that we understand well. How does this happen? Can anything be done to avoid these exasperating experiences?

First, we must recognize that although interpersonal misunderstandings are among the more frustrating of life experiences, they are also among the more common. They are, quite simply, a part of the human condition. Shakespeare's *Romeo and Juliet* was written four hundred years ago, but the tragic misunderstanding that marks the climax of that play still captures the imagination of romantics everywhere. In the final act, after mistaking his lover's feigned suicide for the real thing, a grief-stricken Romeo kills himself. Awakening to find her true love dead, Juliet completes the tragedy by taking her own life. Almost four centuries later, in 1934, Clark Gable and Claudette Colbert won Academy Awards for *It Happened One Night,* a story about star-crossed lovers who almost lost their chance at happiness because of a misunderstanding. In 1962 *The Beverly Hillbillies* was introduced to American television viewers and proceeded to become one of the most popular series ever. No small share of the comedy that surrounded the life of the Clampetts was the result of their inability to understand "city ways" and their tendency to act in ways that were consistently misunderstood by the "city folks" of Beverly Hills.

Real-life history is also full of examples of the dramatic and often devastating effects of interpersonal misunderstandings. Historians such as Michael Beschloss, for example, contend that the well-documented Cuban missile crisis of 1962 was the result of a series of misunderstandings between President Kennedy and communist leaders Nikita Khrushchev and Fidel Castro. Beschloss (1991) suggests that the crisis was at least partially rooted in a misinterpretation of comments made by President Kennedy to Khrushchev's son-in-law, Alexei Adzhubei—comments that Khrushchev and Castro took as a signal of the president's intention to invade Cuba.

That nearly devastating misunderstanding led the United States and the Soviet Union to the brink of nuclear war.

Thus, whether in the context of fiction or real life, interpersonal misunderstandings are capable of transforming assurance into apprehension, consternation into comedy, triviality into tragedy. Most of our mistakes in comprehending the actions of others are so inconsequential as to escape notice, yet on occasion they have been important enough to change the course of history. Being misunderstood is always frustrating and sometimes infuriating, and misunderstanding others can lead to embarrassment or serious interpersonal conflict. Perhaps more significant than all the potential consequences of misunderstandings, however, is the fact that their very existence threatens one of the most basic assumptions upon which all of social life is based: the assumption that others will interpret our actions more or less as we intend them. When misunderstandings call this assumption into question, we feel not just embarrassed, frustrated, or angry; we may feel socially paralyzed, not knowing what to do to remedy the situation. Even seemingly inconsequential misunderstandings tend to disrupt the normal flow of interaction, create confusion, and at least momentarily necessitate a refocusing of our attention and redirection of our actions. More serious misunderstandings can damage or destroy entire relationships among co-workers, friends, or loved ones.

Knowing that it is often difficult to make ourselves understood, even to those we know well, we are often tempted to avoid interaction with those who are strange to us. Yet, like it or not, many of us are required on a regular basis to communicate with individuals whose perspective on the world is radically different from our own. In our much talked about global community, human interaction is increasingly characterized by rewards previously unattainable, but also by interpersonal hazards previously unimagined. Life becomes significantly more complex as we attempt to communicate with those who do not share our assumptions about the meaning of events or about what actions are appropriate, even in the most familiar situations. In some settings, a misunderstood comment or gesture can cause the loss of an important business deal; in others, misunderstandings can cause the loss of human lives.

A couple I know recently had an experience in which a series of misunderstandings endangered their lives and the lives of their two-year-old twin sons. As they were driving through an industrial neighborhood on their way home one night, a car pulled up beside them and the driver, with an angry expression on his face, gestured for them to pull over. Interpreting the stranger's actions as hostile, my friends sped up in hopes of losing him. Rather than backing off, the other driver continued to pursue. Convinced that they were in harm's way, my friends drove even faster and more recklessly in order to stay ahead of the "madman" they feared would run them off the road at the first opportunity. This scene was replayed for several miles at higher and higher speeds until finally a police officer spotted the speeding vehicles and pulled them over. As it turned out, the stranger was a security guard who had heard what he thought were shots being fired near the property he was guarding just as my unfortunate friends drove by. He gave chase, assuming that the shots had come from their vehicle. Apparently not seeing the twins in the back seat, he interpreted my friends' refusal to pull over as evidence of their guilt. They in turn interpreted his demand that they do so—and his insistence on chasing them—as evidence of his intent to do them harm.

Although such encounters with strangers can be extremely frightening, for most of us, they are also rare. What is all too common, however, is the feeling of utter dismay that comes from realizing that we have been misunderstood by someone with whom we have time and again shared our innermost thoughts and feelings. Many a major marital dispute has evolved from a minor misunderstanding. Thus, whether in foreign territory or on our own home turf, the possibility of misunderstanding is an ever-present threat to human interaction.

In order to grasp the nature of interpersonal misunderstandings, we must understand the process through which they unfold, and we must understand the importance of the social and cultural contexts in which they take place. Thus, this book is presented in two parts; the first part explores the social and psychological processes that produce misunderstandings, and the second part locates this process within the contexts of interaction between people of different cultural, social-class, racial, and gender identities.

Misunderstanding or Nonunderstanding?

In order to avoid being misunderstood as an author, I need to define a few key terms. First, I will often refer to the people involved in misunderstandings as "actors" and "observers." By *actors* I mean simply anyone whose behavior has been observed or taken note of by others, while *observers* are those who have taken note of the actions of another. Although this is an important distinction, it is also important to remember that, as interaction proceeds, an individual who is an actor one moment is an observer the next, and vice versa. Thus when I speak of "interactants," I mean individuals who pass the roles of actor and observer back and forth in a sometimes orderly but usually sloppy, inexact, and overlapping manner.

Because this book is about problems of understanding, it is especially important to clearly distinguish between the terms *misunderstanding* and *nonunderstanding*. Misunderstandings exist when observers think they understand the intentions of actors but do not. Nonunderstandings exist when observers realize that they do not understand the actions of others. Thus the primary difference between nonunderstanding and misunderstanding is that when we do not understand the actions of the other we are aware of that fact, whereas when we misunderstand, we don't realize it. I could not claim to have ever misunderstood the nuances of quantum mechanics, for example, because I cannot claim to have ever understood them. This distinction is clear from the way we talk about such things in everyday life. Comments such as "I don't understand" or "I misunderstood" make perfectly good sense to those familiar with our language, but the phrase "I misunderstand" is likely to be taken as a grammatical mistake. These usages imply that, as observers, we can be aware of our misunderstanding of others only as a condition of the past. "I now realize that I *misunderstood* the lecture on quantum mechanics." As actors, however, it is quite possible for us to be aware that we are being misunderstood even as it is happening. "You don't understand what I'm trying to tell you," said the physics professor. The way such problems typically are handled is influenced by the fact that observers can be aware of their misunderstanding of others only after the fact, whereas actors can become aware that their actions are being misunderstood as it is happening. I will pursue this point in more detail later.

Misunderstanding As Process

As the definitions above suggest, we normally think of misunderstandings as states of being that exist when two people have different understandings of what one of them has done or said. However, because the primary purpose of this book is to describe how such states come about, it will be necessary for us to view misunderstandings as dynamic processes. Analyzing them in this way requires that we focus on four possible stages that together constitute the misunderstanding process: (1) an initial action, (2) an observation of that action, (3) an interpretation of what has been observed, and, often but not always, (4) an overt reaction on the part of the observer. Misunderstanding can result from problems at any of these stages. One of the advantages of realizing that misunderstandings are part of an ongoing process of interaction is that we are encouraged to attend to the roles of both actors and observers. Doing so should make us somewhat less defensive regarding our own actions, less judgmental of the actions of others, and consequently better able to work together to overcome the conflicts that often accompany misunderstandings.

I will discuss each of the stages in this process in detail, starting with an analysis of action in the next chapter. Although I will start by considering the types of actions that are most often misunderstood, it is important to

UNDERSTANDING

recognize at the outset that misunderstandings are rarely exclusively the result of flawed or incompetent performances of actors. When we realize the diverse meanings that the same words and deeds can have in different settings, it becomes obvious that actions are given meaning by those who interpret them. It is also true, however, that action plays an important role in the creation of some misunderstandings. We often say things we don't mean or fail to adequately express what we want to say. Sometimes we say too much, sometimes too little.

Although many misunderstandings can be attributed to slips of the tongue or other inappropriate or unexpected actions, many others are the result of observers' errors in seeing or hearing. Does this mean, as is often suggested, that we only hear what we want to hear and see what we want to see? Research from cognitive psychology suggests that it would be more accurate to say that we *can* see only what we *expect* to see. People often have rather rigid expectations of how others should behave, and those expectations get in the way of their seeing or hearing what is actually expressed. This is called "selective perception."

I recently had a personal experience with this problem. While I was having dinner with a group of colleagues, one member of the group turned to the man sitting directly across the table from me and asked him about his research. Knowing him primarily as a specialist in criminology and deviant behavior, I heard his response as, "I've been studying strippers." As he proceeded to describe the coastal town and people he was studying, I found it increasingly difficult to make sense of what he was saying; most of it seemed to have nothing to do with nude dancers. Finally, realizing that I must have misunderstood, I interrupted him and asked, "Did you say you were studying strippers?" He laughed and replied, "No, shrimpers." My categorization of him as someone who studied unusual and illicit behavior had led me to mishear what he had said. This kind of selective perception happens all the time, and often those affected never realize it has happened. Not only what we hear, but also what we see is susceptible to selective perception. In the chapter on observation I will explain how and why such distortions occur.

We humans have a tremendous curiosity about the world around us. As curious creatures, we are rarely satisfied to simply observe; we also have a need to understand why things are as they are. This means that we are continually engaged in the process of interpretation. Even on those rare occasions when we are not particularly curious about the meaning of the other's behavior, our ability to carry on a conversation or formulate appropriate responses to others requires that we accurately interpret the actions we observe. The fact that interpretation is a necessary and frequent activity, however, does not mean that it is easy or that we are always successful at it. In fact, interpretation is even more vulnerable than observation to the contaminating effects of our preconceptions and expectations.

Interpretation is a complicated process because it may involve deciphering not only what was said but why it was said. The most casual greeting between two acquaintances, for example, can raise such questions in our minds as, "Why did he smile that way?" or, "Is he hiding something from me?" Often, misunderstandings are the result of observers imputing more serious or deeper meaning to actions than the actor intended. Those in supervisory positions, for example, are often surprised to find that their most casual comments are assumed by subordinates to carry some deep and ominous meaning. It is all too easy to read too much into, and thus overinterpret, such acts as a casual smile or an unenthusiastic greeting. Of course, it also works the other way around: observers sometimes underinterpret or attribute less significance to actions than actors intend, which leads actors to such erroneous conclusions as, "She never takes me seriously!"

Once behavior has been observed and interpreted, we are usually expected to react in some way. It is at this stage that observers become actors and respond to the initial action on the basis of what they have observed and how they have interpreted it. Of course, not all reactions involve an overt acknowledgment of the misinterpreted action. For example, if we perceive that we have been ignored, snubbed, or insulted, our reaction might well be to ignore it for the time being, either because we are unsure of our interpretation and are thus awaiting additional information or because we simply are not sure how to respond. Whether dramatic or subtle, reactions reflect observers' interpretations of the original action. If our interpretation has been substantially off the mark, our reaction is quite likely to be misinterpreted as well. This is why one misunderstanding so often leads to another. The ease with which misunderstandings escalate and multiply complicates efforts to sort out the truth to everyone's satisfaction. Thus the initial reactions of observers are critical in determining whether a misunderstanding is cleared up, continues, or escalates into a series of misunderstandings or a serious conflict. The following account, provided by one of my former students, illustrates the point.

> Two friends had a misunderstanding about money. Susan owed Linda money for a phone bill. Susan sent a check in the mail to Linda. Linda claims not to have received it. Susan sends another check. Linda claims not to have received it either, and then accuses Susan of lying. Linda then writes a letter to Susan telling her she wishes to end their friendship. Of course, Linda was not very polite about this. Susan receives the first check back, stamped "Return to Sender." Susan makes no effort to resolve the situation, feeling that Linda has shown her no trust. Linda still thinks Susan lied about the checks and Susan still thinks Linda is trying to obtain extra money dishonestly.

Because conflicts of this sort are so often byproducts of misunderstanding, it is important to consider how we typically try to avoid conflict or defuse it when it does occur. One strategy that is frequently used is to acknowledge that a misunderstanding has occurred and let that acknowledgment stand as an explanation for the conflict. This strategy is so successful in repairing damaged interactions that it is often employed even when misunderstandings have not occurred. By agreeing to attribute conflicts to misunderstanding, interactants are able to get on with the business at hand and avoid serious damage to their personal relationship. Perhaps most importantly, such *misunderstanding accounts* accomplish these things without either party having to assume sole responsibility for the original conflict, thus allowing everyone to save face. I will discuss the use of misunderstanding accounts in more detail in the chapter on reaction.

Contexts of Misunderstandings

The second part of this book is devoted to an examination of the cultural and interpersonal contexts of misunderstandings. In considering the role of culture in the creation of misunderstanding, I will focus primarily on problems associated with intercultural communication. Differences in language and the meaning of nonverbal gestures pose especially difficult problems for those attempting to communicate across cultural boundaries. Because such problems are not unique to international communication, however, my analysis will also include problems of understanding across American ethnic and social class groups. In his book *Black and White Styles in Conflict,* for example, Thomas Kochman reveals how cultural differences produce different interactional styles that often produce misunderstandings and unnecessary conflicts when whites and African Americans discuss serious issues.

Although ethnic diversity has characterized America's largest cities for decades, today even our small towns and rural areas are increasingly comprised of people who trace their origins to the far corners of the globe. Mexican, Vietnamese, Indian, and numerous other ethnic enclaves have become familiar parts of both urban and rural communities throughout America's heartland. Although we may eat at the same restaurants, shop in the same stores, and send our kids to the same schools, communication with each other across ethnic boundaries tends to be superficial and is often punctuated by misunderstanding. Failure to understand the cultural practices of those around us is often a source of serious conflict. The following excerpt from a newspaper article illustrates this problem.

> Since the 1992 Los Angeles riots—a traumatic event in the collective experience of 1 million Koreans in the United States—a lot of effort has gone into helping immi-

grants avoid the behavior that is often misinterpreted by those unfamiliar with their culture. To be sure, many factors contributed to the targeting of Korean American-owned businesses during the riots. Korean leaders in Los Angeles readily acknowledge that unpleasant encounters had occurred between Korean shopkeepers and their customers. But, they believe, the negative media portrayal of Korean shopkeepers as rude and uncaring people—without adequate response from Korean proprietors—was the main reason why Koreans were singled out in the looting and firebombing during the riots ... Though they feel strongly that this media-reinforced stereotype was unfair, their frustration has propelled thoughtful Korean Americans to come together to try to climb over the cultural wall that has made Koreans perhaps the most misunderstood of Asian immigrants. "When you get to know Koreans, you'll find them compassionate, kind and loyal," said Mr. Hong. But Koreans neither toot their horn nor go out of their way to make it easy for outsiders to get to know them, he says ... Smiling, saying "hello" and shaking hands may be natural to most Americans, but they are not for Korean immigrants in whose culture a smile and small talk are usually reserved for friends and families—and from their point of view, not to be squandered on strangers. Though displaying emotions may not be a virtue in his culture, businessman Jimmy Park has taken to heart the old adage about doing what Romans do when you're in Rome ... Mr. Park says Koreans definitely should smile more and lower their voices. "Koreans have loud voices," he said. That, combined with dour faces and limited English, can lead to miscommunication. (Dallas Morning News, *October 23, 1994*)

Americans who do business overseas also have learned the economic value of acquiring some understanding of the cultures of countries where they do business. Such a multicultural approach to business is increasingly necessary, even for those who are not required to conduct negotiations beyond the borders of their own communities. In fact, those who make the effort are finding that investments in intercultural understanding have direct payoffs in the form of better business with fewer problems and indirect payoffs in the form of more congenial work environments.

The way we behave and the way we interpret each other's behavior is also influenced by the formal relationships that link us to each other. For example, in most societies, our own included, who is allowed to act familiar with whom depends largely on the relative power of the individuals involved. An individual in a position of power is typically allowed to act in a more familiar way than someone in a subordinate position. Thus, although an employer might be quite comfortable asking personal questions of his or her employees, the opposite is rarely true. In a more general sense, all interaction is constrained by the social roles we assume in relation to each other. In the second part of the book, which deals with the cultural and social contexts of misunderstandings, I will pay special attention to the kinds of problems that emerge in informal interactions with family and friends and those that are typically experienced in formal work settings, especially misunderstandings that are linked to differences in formal power.

The gender of those involved is another important factor in defining the social context of interactions. Numerous books have been published in recent years dealing with male–female communication problems. Sociolinguist Deborah Tannen (1990) suggests that men and women often misunderstand what the other wants or needs because they fail to understand the unspoken implications of the other's way of saying things. In a sense, boys and girls grow up in different worlds—worlds that have been largely shaped by adults. As they mature, however, they must learn to forge their own unique relationships with members of the opposite sex. Eventually, most of us unite with a member of the other sex and begin the difficult job of cooperatively constructing a shared life. Nothing in our socialization experience adequately prepares us for that task and, as a result, interaction between women and men attempting to construct a shared and mutually satisfactory life is fraught with confusion and misunderstanding. Women and men who must work together face similar difficulties in creating and sustaining mutual understanding. Thus, in the final chapter I will discuss the role of gender in the misunderstanding process.

Avoiding and Handling Misunderstandings

In addition to explaining some aspects of how misunderstandings come about, the following chapters include specific recommendations and techniques that might aid in the avoidance and resolution of misunderstandings. Although I hope some of my suggestions will prove helpful, I suspect that the greater benefit will come from understanding more fully why and how misunderstandings occur. It would be both pretentious and untrue to suggest that reading this book will in any way assure that those who read it will never again misunderstand nor be misunderstood, or that it will spare them the discomfort, confusion, or conflicts that often result when misunderstandings do occur. However, to the extent that knowledge is power, understanding misunderstandings should be of benefit to anyone who wishes to more smoothly negotiate the rugged and often confusing terrain of everyday social life.

PART ONE

THE PROCESS OF MISUNDERSTANDING

CHAPTER
T
W
O

2 Action

The Problem

of Being

Misunderstood

*Republicans understand the importance of
bondage between mother and child.*[1]

DAN QUAYLE, *former Vice President*

*This isn't a man who is leaving with
his head between his legs.*

DAN QUAYLE, *when asked
about then Chief of Staff John Sununu's resignation*

Although my dog Jack can't talk, he is—unlike most politicians—a master of clear and concise communication. When he comes to me and puts both paws in my lap, he needs one of two things, either more water in his bowl or a trip outside to relieve himself of the water that was in his bowl. Figuring out which is simple. I check his water bowl, and if it is not empty I take him outside. If he crouches down on his belly, looks at me intently until he gets my attention, then springs up and moves toward the front door while looking back at me, he wants to go outside to visit his girlfriend's yard, down the street. If he sits by the dining room table intently watching us eat . . . well, I guess that one is universally understood. Even though Jack is capable of the occasional ruse, such as when he barks an alarm not because he sees or hears something outside but because he is trying to trick us into getting up and paying him some attention, for the most part he means what he barks and barks what he means. Too bad the same can't be said of people.

It is slightly ironic that we humans with our sophisticated brains and elaborate languages so often fail to get our points across, even when they are quite simple points. I say slightly ironic because it is clear that our ability to be indirect, deceitful, sarcastic, or ironic—as well as straightforward, honest, or literal—makes the job of interpreting the actions of other people much more complicated than deciphering the intentions of our pets. Unfortunately, this not only makes it harder to understand others, but it also makes it harder to formulate our own actions without having them misinterpreted.

Little Actions, Big Acts

I used to play golf. I started playing in college after becoming friends with three guys on my university's golf team. In fact, I shared an apartment with them for a year. As a result of hanging around with them, watching them play in matches, and occasionally playing a round with them, I learned a great deal about the game. Although I never played enough to get very good, I learned enough to become convinced that I could watch someone hit a ball and pretty accurately diagnose any major problems with his or her swing. Unfortunately, this sometimes got me into trouble with friends, with whom I was only too willing to share my observations about why they were slicing, hooking, or topping the ball. I welcomed such comments from others regarding my own play and always intended my suggestions not as criticisms but as genuine attempts to help them improve their game, and they were usually taken that way. Occasionally, however, it was clear that my observations were not welcome and were seen as unwarranted criticism—unwarranted not necessarily because my partner's play needed no improvement, and only partly because my own performance hardly recommended me as an authority on the subject of hitting a golf ball. A large part of the problem was simple, yet easily overlooked. Usually when we take action we know the intention of our actions before they are completed, but when we observe others we must interpret their actions after the fact, strictly on the basis of what we see and hear. Because I knew that my golf-related comments were intended to be helpful rather than critical, it was hard for me to see or hear my actions as they were being perceived by others. For this reason, observers are often likely to interpret actions in ways that actors find incomprehensible.

For the purpose of analyzing social interaction, sociologist Alfred Schutz (1971) distinguishes between *acts* and *actions*. In essence, actions are the words and deeds that go into a completed act. For example, the act of greeting someone might be accomplished through the three actions of smiling, saying "hello," and extending our hand to shake theirs. All these actions have a specific meaning for the actor before they take place, but they are meaningful to the observer only after they have been completed and interpreted. The act of making a friendly suggestion about another's golf swing might consist of the actions of putting a hand on the other's shoulder and saying something like, "You know, you have a good swing, but on that kind of shot you might want to shorten your back swing a bit." Because the actor who makes such a suggestion knows his intention before he acts, he will see each of the individual actions as part of and consistent with the total act. Thus, it is unlikely that he will realize that the hand on the shoulder might be taken as a gesture of condescension rather than affection. However, the golfer who has just made the bad shot must interpret each of the other's actions without knowing either the other's intention or what actions are to follow. As a result, the hand on the shoulder might be interpreted negatively and generate bad feelings before the more positive words are ever heard. Because at that moment the observer is likely to be feeling a bit incompetent, the "suggestion" that he do it differently next time might well be interpreted as an act of condescension from someone who feels superior. Any actions that are inconsistent with the intended act are capable of undermining the actor's overall intent. The individual actions that cumulatively create a completed act may consist of both verbal and nonverbal actions. Studies of nonverbal communication reveal that our nonverbal actions often undermine our verbal ones (Mehrabian 1981). Sometimes this is intentional, such as when we insult a friend while making it clear that the insult is intended to be in jest by smiling or using body language to convey that we are not being serious. Sometimes it is unintentional, however, such as when our facial expression gives away our disappointment or disapproval even as our words express happiness or approval.

Generating an entire set of actions that are consistent with an intended act is often difficult, yet it can be vital to maintaining credibility, especially when our actions are being closely scrutinized. Politicians increasingly struggle with this problem when they are called upon to explain past actions that are inconsistent with the public image they wish to maintain. In offering such explanations, they must be careful to insure that their accounts are sufficient to ease public concerns without sounding too much like made-up excuses or justifications. When their explanations become too elaborate, they run the risk of making a single comment that could destroy the overall credibility of their message. On March 29, 1992, presidential candidate Bill Clinton, appearing at a candidate's forum on WCBS-TV in New York, was asked whether he had ever taken illegal drugs. According to a *New York Times* article the next day, his response was as follows: "I've never broken a state law, but when I was in England I experimented with marijuana a time or two, and I didn't like it. I didn't inhale it, and never tried it again." Clinton explained that this had happened at a party where numerous Oxford students were smoking. This revelation probably didn't shock anyone. After all, it had occurred many years before at a time and in a place where many if not most people his age were doing the same thing. It appeared to many observers, however, that the candidate had overstepped the bounds of credibility in claiming not to have inhaled. Whether people believed him or not, that single comment became the source of numerous jokes in the succeeding weeks.

The act of admitting or explaining a transgression, or apologizing for one's behavior, as in Clinton's case, usually consists of a number of individual actions. These actions include individual comments (such as "I didn't inhale") plus changes in tone of voice, various nonverbal gestures, facial expressions, and so forth. Knowing where he was going with his explanation before his listeners did, Mr. Clinton is likely to have seen each comment in his statement as consistent with his overall intention of making what would be heard as a frank admission. In fact, his listeners appeared to have been willing to accept his overall explanation that his marijuana experience or experiences had been isolated and understandable within the social context in which they occurred. However, because his listeners did not know whether they were hearing an honest admission or another attempt by a politician at what has come to be known as "damage control," many perceived the comment that he did not inhale as a roundabout way of denying that he had really smoked pot, even as he was in the process of admitting, by most definitions, that he had.

No matter what we are doing, in order to be convincing, we must convey the impression that our actions are consistent with our overall intention. An apology that is delivered in a tone of voice that does not suggest that the speaker is really sorry is not likely to be heard as sincere. Likewise, a threat that is delivered in a quivering voice is not likely to intimidate. Big acts are made up of lots of little actions, each of which is capable of producing a misunderstanding of our overall intent.

It is important to remember that despite our best intentions, and no matter how obvious they may be to us, the real reasons for our acts are not always obvious to others. Thinking back over the individual actions that went into the overall act might help us realize that a single word or gesture which to us seemed very minor played a major part in the creation of a misunderstanding. In conflict situations, this kind of realization will help defuse our own frustration and anger and pave the way for a resolution of the problem. In some cases, explicitly stating what our intentions were and were not is helpful, but as we shall see in the next section, knowing when to pursue the issue and when to let it rest is also important.

When to Act: Emotion and the Importance of Timing

The way we interpret a particular action is closely linked to our emotional state at the time. As a result, misunderstandings sometimes occur because we misidentify the sources of our arousal. If I make a mistake and someone points it out, I may feel angry, but am I angry with myself for making the mistake or with the other for pointing it out? More fundamentally, is it anger I feel, or is it embarrassment? Social psychologist Stanley Schachter says that all emotional experience is the result of a two-stage process. In the first stage we feel the effects of physiological arousal (quickened heart rate, sweaty palms, etc.), and in the second stage we attempt to find an appropriate explanation for it. The problem is, we frequently mistake one emotion for another, which may lead us to confuse such feelings as fear and anger.

In order to test Schachter's theory, Dutton and Aron designed a study to assess the ability of men to accurately identify the source of their feelings in an emotionally arousing situation. As part of their study, a woman approached several groups of men who were visiting a park in British Columbia, explained to them that she was conducting research on the effect of scenic attractions on creativity, and asked them to answer a questionnaire. One group of men was approached as they were walking across a narrow 450-foot-long expansion bridge suspended 200 feet over a raging rocky river, an experience most people would find highly arousing. A second group of men was approached after they had made it across the bridge and had had time to rest and calm down from the exhilarating experience. After handing them the questionnaire, the woman said she would be happy to explain the research in more detail later when she had more time. She then wrote down her name and phone number and handed it to the subjects. According to Schachter's (1964) theory, the men who encountered the woman on the bridge when they were physiologically aroused would be more likely to attribute their feelings of arousal to the woman and thus feel more attracted to her. Consistent with the theory, Dutton and Aron (1974) found that 65 percent of the men who met the woman on the bridge at the height of their physiological arousal later called and asked her for a date, whereas only 30 percent of those who met her after crossing the bridge did so. Numerous other studies show similar results. These studies also reveal that, no matter why people are aroused, other people who happen to be present at the time of the arousal are likely to be seen as its primary cause.

If people are prone to misidentify the source of their emotional arousal, it is clear that we should closely monitor our actions around those who are aroused, no matter what the reason for their state. It is probably best not to offer advice to those who are upset about their performance—whether on the golf course, in the kitchen, or at work—until they have had time to calm down. I now realize that my friendly advice to my golfing buddies back in college, if nothing else, was poorly timed. Had I waited until after their frustration had subsided, they probably would not have associated my advice with the negative emotions they were feeling. Clearly, there is a time to speak and a time to keep quiet. Knowing when to act is often as important as knowing what to do in avoiding misunderstandings.

Good timing also involves being aware of the emotional state of those we are interacting with and taking that into consideration in formulating our responses. It is when the other is emotionally upset that we are most likely to feel the need to make helpful suggestions. However, that is not always the best time for such suggestions. A husband, for example, may try to suggest ways of solving the problem that has his wife upset, only to have her become more frustrated. This in turn frustrates the husband, which makes bad matters worse. Often, when others are upset, it is best to simply offer a sympathetic ear, saving our suggestions until they have had time to reach a state of emotional stability.

Did I Really Slay That? On Freudian Slips

Perhaps the most basic requirement for being understood is saying what we intend to say. Simple slips of the tongue are thus an important source of misunderstandings. One of the most popular explanations for slips of the tongue is that sometimes when we speak we have two competing motives or intentions. The first motive determines what we consciously wish to say while the second, of which we may not be aware, competes with the first and distorts the expression of it. This explanation is so closely identified with the psychoanalytic interpretations of Sigmund Freud (1965) that such mistakes have come to be known as "Freudian slips." Although sexually suggestive slips are the types most often identified as "Freudian," they constitute a small portion (approximately one quarter) of those analyzed and discussed by Freud.

Freud's theory of speech errors is both fascinating and provocative. Unfortunately, his explanation for slips of the tongue—like many of his other ideas—is untestable. Since the subconscious cannot be observed or measured, there is no way to scientifically study how it works. One approach to assessing his theory, however, is to ask whether there are other, perhaps more simple and more testable, explanations for some of the slips Freud attributes to the subconscious.

Consider the following slip of the tongue by New York Congresswoman Bella Abzug, who was addressing a rally for the Equal Rights Amendment at the time: "We need laws that protect everyone. Men and women, straights and gays, regardless of sexual perversion . . . ah, persuasion . . ." A Freudian interpretation of this slip would be that, her public pronouncements not withstanding, Ms. Abzug secretly or subconsciously considered gays to be sexual perverts. However, there is an explanation that is both simpler and more consistent with other information about the speaker. First, in our culture the terms *sexual* and *perversion* are so commonly linked that we are somewhat conditioned to expect the one to follow the other. Second, errant word substitutions are much more likely if the words sound alike, such as *perversion* and *persuasion*. This explanation, which does not depend on the assumed existence of dark, mysterious, or subconscious motives on the part of the speaker, is supported by considerable linguistic research.

Here is another example from the precarious world of political speech making. Referring to Senator Hubert Humphrey in a speech to the 1980 Democratic National Convention, then President Jimmy Carter said: "I am speaking of a great man who should have been President and would have been one of the greatest Presidents in history—Herbert Horatio Hornblower." Did President Carter consider Senator Humphrey a political hornblower, a slang term originally used to describe those who engage in hard-sell advertising? Did he secretly consider Humphrey a person who was inclined to "blow his own horn?" Or was this simply a linguistic substitution that resulted from Carter's familiarity with C. S. Forester's fictitious British naval officer Horatio Hornblower? This is likely, given the fact that Carter himself had served in the Navy. Moreover, like most speakers, Carter probably was not accustomed to including Humphrey's middle name in references to him. If so, the name Horatio would most likely be connected in his memory with Hornblower rather than Humphrey. Given Carter's admiration for Humphrey, it seems more plausible that his slip of the tongue was of a linguistic rather than a Freudian nature. Of course, there is no way to know for certain when slips of the tongue are linguistic and when they are Freudian. However, most linguists would argue that, although some slips of this sort may be the result of unconscious motives, it is likely that most are of a much more innocent origin. As Freud himself might have put it, sometimes a slip of the tongue is just a cigar.

Slips of the tongue are a common part of talk. Sometimes they are funny, sometimes embarrassing, and sometimes they create troublesome misunderstandings. Realizing that even sexually suggestive or potentially insulting slips often are the product of linguistic limitations rather than dark unconscious motives should make us less suspicious of those who make such mistakes and less embarrassed when we make them ourselves. After all, the more certain we are that our mistakes are innocent, the less guilty we are likely to appear.

Choosing Our Words: The Uses and Misuses of Irony and Sarcasm

Often we are misunderstood not for failing to say what we intend to say but for choosing the wrong way to express our ideas. Teachers, politicians, and others who speak in public settings must not only choose carefully what to say and what not to say, but also be concerned with how they say it. Those who fail to address their comments at a level appropriate to their audience run the risk of either losing the audience altogether or having their message misunderstood. Over the years, I have heard quite a few college professors express frustration because their students misunderstood them, in many cases inferring the exact opposite of what they had intended to communicate. I eventually came to the conclusion that their problems were often the result of misunderstood sarcasm or irony. Although irony and sarcasm can be used to liven up otherwise boring talk, these devices can backfire if listeners interpret them literally. The following example was provided by a colleague.

> The other day I was lecturing on the idea of cultural capital. In order to illustrate the point, I had the class calculate their own cultural capital scores. They were to add certain points if their parents had college degrees or were professionals, if they had traveled abroad, etc. Then I said, sarcastically, "Since we all know that women and blacks are worth less than men and whites, deduct five points if you are female and five more if you are black." The next day, the department chair told me that a student had come by to complain that I had said in class that blacks and women were inferior to white men.

Most of the time people have little trouble understanding the meaning of ironic statements. For example, if someone says "smooth move" to a waiter who has just spilled a plate of spaghetti on the white dress of a customer, most people realize that the statement is not intended to be taken literally. In fact, it seems that such sarcasm is usually intended to convey the opposite of what is said. Psycholinguists such as Dan Sperber and D. Wilson (1981), however, point out that speakers often use ironic statements not necessarily to imply the opposite, but to ridicule the idea and anyone who would believe it. In doing so, speakers implicitly express their own disapproval of the expressed idea. Thus, when a parent sarcastically responds to the sounds emanating from their teenager's stereo with "great music!" they may be expressing both the opinion that the music is terrible and the idea that they disapprove of their offspring for liking it.

Whether we assume a statement is intended literally, ironically, or sarcastically will depend on our assessment of the speaker. "Great music" will be taken to mean "terrible music" only if the teenager already knows or assumes that the parent hates that kind of music. Steve, a white student from the South, and Thomas, an African American student from the Midwest, got into an argument in class because of a comment Steve made during a class discussion. In commenting on race relations, Steve had made use of a negative stereotype of African Americans in what he intended to be an ironic expression of disapproval of those who think that way. Partly because Steve spoke with a southern accent, however, Thomas interpreted the ironic comment literally, and was offended by it. It is clear from these examples that the effective use of sarcasm or irony is difficult, and unless we are certain of how our audience perceives us, using either of these modes of expression can be risky business. Because irony and sarcasm usually require that we say the opposite of what we mean, they are more likely than perhaps any other type of comment to produce misunderstandings.

The use of sarcasm varies quite a bit from one cultural group to another. Adults are also more capable of understanding irony and sarcasm than are children. It is probably best to avoid the use of irony to convey the opposite of what you say if your audience might be inclined to associate you, or your social group, with the literal meaning. For example, it is probably unwise to attempt to mock or condemn male chauvinism by making mock sexist comments. Both men who are actively chauvinistic and women who are extremely sensitive to the issue may not notice that your tongue is in your cheek, especially if you are a man.

Meaning What We Don't Say and Saying What We Don't Mean

Although mistakes in speech are an obvious source of misunderstanding, even without them the subtleties of talk are staggeringly complex and easily misunderstood. For example, take the common habit of being indirect. Although some people have raised the use of indirect speech to an art, we all employ this device as a way of saying what we want without having to say it in so many words. When we want to eat, rather than simply stating, "I want to eat as soon as possible," most of us are inclined to use a more indirect comment, such as, "I'm hungry." Statements of this sort are especially deceptive because on the surface they are quite direct. However, because they imply more than they state, they can be a source of confusion. One of the obvious advantages of indirection is that if we are called to task for what we have implied, we can deny it. "No, I didn't mean we have to eat now, I was just feeling a little hungry." Even more indirect utterances, such as, "How long has it been since we ate lunch?" allow us to plant a seed without actually making a request or a demand.

The use of indirect speech allows us to hedge our bets. However, it will be effective only if used for communicating to an audience capable of understanding and appreciating such subtleties. In keeping with the overall pace of life, the speech of urban Americans, especially those from the Northeast, tends to be fast and direct, whereas the speech of those from rural areas and southern states tends to be slower and more indirect. These differences have produced stereotypical images of northeasterners as rude and southerners as overtly friendly but covertly devious. Despite such subtle differences, most Americans—regardless of region—tend to communicate rather precisely and explicitly. This style of communication stands in stark contrast to the more implicit style of the Japanese. According to Diana Rowland (1993), expert on Japanese business etiquette, in Japan the most important part of a message is likely to be communicated in such a subtle and indirect way that Americans can easily conclude the opposite of what is meant. Unless we understand such fundamental differences, those who use an implicit style of communication will often appear vague and insincere to their more explicit counterparts, while those who are more explicit might appear brash and self-centered to anyone unaccustomed to their manner.

However, even in an explicit culture such as that of the United States, "spitting out" exactly what we mean does not guarantee that we will be understood the way we want. No matter how direct and explicit we try to be, casual conversation is full of unspoken assumptions about what the hearer already knows and, therefore, is expected to fill in. Most utterances are somewhat cryptic; we rarely say precisely that we mean. In fact, treating what another says in its most literal sense is often used as a form of humor. A moment ago, my daughter came over to where I was sitting and asked, "Dad, do you have a pen or pencil?" Had I taken her question literally or chosen to answer it that way I might have replied with a simple "yes," but as I was not in the mood to be sarcastic I pointed to my book bag and said, "Look under the flap." Rather than interpreting her question literally and without filling in the gaps, I took it to mean: "Dad, do you have a pen or pencil with you that I may borrow, and may I borrow it now?" Likewise, it was not necessary for me to say, "Yes, I have a pen with me that you may borrow, and if you look under the flap of my book bag you will find it." A simple point of the finger did the trick.

Such cryptic and imprecise communication is more than just convenient. Because of the assumption of shared knowledge and experience that underlies it, communication of this sort creates a sense of solidarity and connection between those who use it. Shared experiences are the stuff of which relationships are made. Notice how often old friends rely on lengthy remember-the-time conversations to renew intimacy. The use of more precise (often heard as formal) speech tends to distance speakers from their audiences. Moreover, because this function of everyday talk is so common and taken for granted, we notice it only when someone deviates from the normal pattern. To illustrate just how disruptive it can be when someone fails to employ shared background assumptions in everyday conversation, sociologist Harold Garfinkel asked his students to try and suspend such assumptions in their own talk at home and to refuse to allow them when others spoke. The "experiment" proved difficult and resulted in angry, shocked, and bewildered friends and relatives. The following conversation is one of the examples Garfinkel (1967:43) cites (S refers to the subject and E to the experimenter/student).

"On Friday night my husband and I were watching television. My husband remarked that he was tired. I asked, 'How are you tired? Physically, mentally, or just bored?'"

S: I don't know, I guess physically, mainly.
E: You mean that your muscles ache or your bones?
S: I guess so. Don't be so technical.
   (*after more watching*)
S: All these old movies have the same kind of old iron bedstead in them.
E: What do you mean? Do you mean all old movies, or some old movies, or just the ones you have seen?
S: What's the matter with you? You know what I mean.
E: I wish you would be more specific.
S: You know what I mean! Drop dead!

In this case the husband was not using his first comment as a way of seeking medical advice; thus he neither understood nor appreciated his wife's probing. Similarly, his second comment about old movie beds was not intended as an introduction to an in-depth analysis of the issue. He was simply sharing a thought, as we often do, for the purpose of creating a connection with the other person. The frustration of the husband illustrates how dependent we are on the willingness and ability of others to fill in the gaps of our talk by mentally referring to our shared pasts. Shared experiences provide a context for the interpretation of current actions. Although reliance on background assumptions is a necessary aspect of normal communication, it is this very feature of everyday talk that often leads to misunderstanding. In order to be understood, speakers must provide enough information to allow others to apply the appropriate interpretive contexts.

Knowing how much to assume is often difficult. Talk that assumes too much may presume a closeness that the listener is not prepared to accept. Women sometimes complain that strangers, both male and female, are more likely to presume a level of intimacy with them that they do not assume with men. This may be done by referring to women they have just met by their first names or asking them personal questions. Regardless of their intentions, such actions are likely to be interpreted as presumptuous and indicating a lack of respect.

On the other hand, a reluctance to rely on shared background knowledge may create the impression that the speaker wishes to maintain distance between himself and his audience. A friend I have known for years and with whom I have shared a variety of experiences does this on the telephone. Despite the fact that we now live hundreds of miles apart and rarely see each other, we still immediately recognize each other's voice on the phone. Yet, whenever he calls, he identifies himself with his full name. I find that somewhat disconcerting because it makes me feel that we have lost touch. Although I know that is not his intention, it always takes a few moments of talk before I am convinced that our relationship is still on familiar ground. Thus, in addition to creating ambiguity about what we mean, speech that assumes too little can also create undesired distance between speaker and audience.

Being too direct or familiar can be offensive and being too indirect or distant can appear evasive or uncaring. In situations of high uncertainty our only option may be to choose in which direction we are willing to err, and that choice should be made only after careful consideration of both our short-term and our long-term goals. Remember, behavior that works well in business dealings may not be well received in less formal settings, and vice versa.

If the purpose of talk were simply to convey information, perhaps we would be more precise. But it is clear that talk is also a primary way of expressing who we are and how we are connected to each other. Being able to express a lot by saying a little—or perhaps nothing—increases our sense of connection with those around us. Calling up shared experiences by merely uttering a simple word or phrase brings us closer together, reminds us of what has been shared, and expresses a desire to maintain intimacy or connection. We would find it both frustrating and alienating to have to articulate precisely what we meant every time we spoke, and doing so would undermine one of the main reasons we interact. Thus, given the inherently ambiguous nature of human communication, the benefits of maintaining personal connection and ease of interaction may be worth the price of an occasional misunderstanding.

Saying Is Doing

The idea that talk can be used to create social bridges or gulfs between speakers and audiences suggests that when we talk we do more than just communicate ideas. In order to be understood, therefore, speakers must be careful about what they are doing with their words. For example, the exact meaning of an utterance such as "Nick will be late" cannot be known until we know whether the speaker is stating a fact or announcing a prediction. Whether the statement means Nick *will* be late or Nick *probably will* be late depends on whether Nick has reported to the speaker that he is running late or whether, on the basis of other information or previous experience, the speaker is predicting that Nick will be late. The meaning of such a statement is often made clear by other events. If the speaker says "Nick will be late" immediately after hanging up the phone from a conversation with Nick, it is reasonable to assume that his comment is a statement of fact. On the other hand, if the statement is made in the context of a conversation about Nick's general unreliability, it would seem to suggest a prediction.

Even such fundamentally different acts as complementing and criticizing can be confused. After getting dressed to go out, Kathie asks Jeff, "How does this look?" Her clothes look nice and appropriate for the occasion, so he responds, "Fine!" Much to his surprise, Kathie snaps back, "You think I look terrible!" What Jeff doesn't understand is that Kathie only asks him to comment on her appearance when she is less than satisfied with it. Thus, anything short of a strong affirmation will be interpreted negatively. Although Jeff may have seen himself as providing an objective assessment of her appearance, what he has actually done by answering "fine" is confirm Kathie's judgment that she looks terrible. Thus, what might have been intended as a minor complement was understood as a criticism.

One of the more important things we do with our choice of words is create an impression of ourselves in the minds of our audience. For example, in addition to clarifying what we are doing, certain prefatory phrases may also create impressions of self that may or may not be desirable. For example, disclaimers such as "I may be wrong, but . . ." are commonly used to introduce comments that might be considered controversial. Although such phrases might effectively ease the impact of what follows, they might also unintentionally create the impression that the speaker lacks confidence, which in turn might prevent others from taking what is said seriously. In general, disclaimers should probably be avoided when we need to appear confident and on top of the situation. On other occasions, however, such as casual conversations with people we do not know well, this same phrase may be taken as an indication of proper humility.

In situations of uncertainty, nothing is an adequate substitute for saying precisely what we are doing when we speak. Phrases such as "I predict," "I believe," "I know," and so on, go a long way toward insuring that whatever follows will be understood accurately. The use of disclaimers such as "I'm no expert, but . . ." may suggest a lack of confidence and should probably be avoided in situations where we need to project an air of confidence. In other situations, however, such phrases may be used successfully to avoid appearing arrogant.

Why Did I Say That? Personality and Misspeaks

One of the most easily observed and intensively studied of human personality characteristics is that of extroversion–introversion. There is by now a fairly convincing body of scientific evidence that some of us are prone to be more active, outgoing, talkative, and excitable than others. Although there are no such things as pure introverts or pure extroverts, some of us have a tendency to be more active, excitable, talkative, and outgoing, whereas others are more calm, laid back, quiet, and solitary. Because of differences in the way their central nervous systems work, outgoing extroverts require higher levels of stimulation than do quieter introverts. Moreover, because they require greater external stimulation, extroverts become easily bored and are more likely to seek out others for social interaction. Being more comfortable at the center of attention, extroverts also tend to do more talking than others. Adrian Furnham (1990) suggests that extroverts also tend to talk faster and be a bit looser with their tongues, often speaking before their ideas are fully formulated. If so, extroverts are also prone to say things in ways that can be easily misinterpreted.

Once a person becomes known as an extrovert, however, he or she can easily become the victim of others' expectations. A normally talkative extroverted person recently confided in me that others often mistakenly assume that she is angry or upset if she does not contribute more than her share to conversations. In fact, a lack of input on her part is more likely the result of her being tired or not feeling well. Nevertheless, in order to avoid misunderstandings, she often feels compelled to talk, even when she would rather remain silent.

Of course all of us, even the quietest of introverts, occasionally say things we immediately or soon thereafter wish we could take back. Even those who have a tendency to be somewhat introverted often feel compelled to respond when spoken to. Two professors from different departments who play softball on the same team saw each other outside their building. As they passed, Tim said to David, "I hear you won't be able to play softball this semester." David confirmed the rumor, explaining that he had a night class at the time their games were scheduled to be played and expressing his disappointment at the situation. Laughing, Tim smiled and said, "Oh well, I'm sure we can lose without you." Without thinking, David replied, "I'm sure you can." What he meant was something like, "Since we often lose when I'm there, I guess it really won't matter if I'm not." Had he thought for a second before responding, that is probably what he would have said. After they parted, however, it occurred to him that Tim might have been suggesting, in his typically wry fashion, that David—one of the better players on the team—would indeed be missed. If so, David's reply might have sounded very conceited, which is certainly not what he had intended.

Thinking back over this story, it occurred to me that highly extroverted individuals probably have the *wish-I-hadn't-said-that* experience quite often. If so, they also have more experience than introverts in dealing with such problems. Moreover, because of a greater need to engage in interaction, extroverts are probably less likely than introverts to avoid individuals with whom they have had misunderstandings.

Interested in knowing whether you would be classified as an extrovert or an introvert? Self-administered tests for those and other personality characteristics can be found in *Please Understand Me* by D. Keirsey and M. Bates (1984). One of the best ways to learn about ourselves is to observe others. From among your acquaintances, identify someone who seems to be an obvious introvert and someone else who seems to be an obvious extrovert. Observe the differences not only in how frequently they interact with others but in the ways they interact and the types of interactional problems they encounter. Does one seem to become involved in misunderstandings more often than the other? Do you notice differences in the way they handle such problems?

Conclusion: Just Because You're Paranoid, That Doesn't Mean You Didn't Screw Up

Even though misunderstanding is something that occurs between people, we most often think of it as the work of individuals: people are sometimes misunderstood and sometimes they misunderstand. This chapter has dealt with just a few of the myriad ways in which our actions can convey meanings that we do not intend. I began by distinguishing between the individual actions that go into a completed act. Looking at behavior in this way makes it clear that conveying the meanings and impressions we intend can be a complex and multistage process in which one slight misstep can alter the overall effect in dramatic ways. Even the most careful planning and coordination of actions in order to insure the right outcome, however, does not guarantee that a minor slip of the tongue or unfortunate choice of words will not completely destroy even the best laid plans. Ironic or sarcastic comments that are interpreted literally are likely to create an impression that is in direct opposition to what we intend, and simple linguistic slips that are attributed to dark unconscious motives can be both embarrassing and destructive of good relations. Likewise, by being indirect and implicit rather than direct and explicit, we run the risk of being misread. Moreover, no matter how carefully we choose our words and how carefully we deliver them, and no matter how carefully we integrate our words with our body language and other forms of nonverbal behavior, we are still vulnerable to the inevitable fact that the same words and deeds can have multiple meanings depending upon the situational context. The same words, such as "tomorrow the rain will stop," can express a firm prediction, a fervent wish, or a sarcastic form of disgust or resignation.

Of course, we can perhaps reduce such errors by stating our purposes with such phrases as "I predict" or "I wish," choosing our words carefully and being more literal with what we say, but such strategies carry their own costs, such as producing unnecessary anxiety on the part of actors and taking much of the fun out of social intercourse for everyone. Moreover, because of basic personality differences, some of us are less capable than others of such a methodical approach to interaction. Those who thrive on social interaction and are energized by the presence of others might find it more difficult to hold back and think before speaking. Inevitably such individuals, especially extroverts, will occasionally say too much, speak too quickly, or act in ways they later regret. After all, no matter how precise, politic, or articulate we might be, the more often we act, the more often we run the risk of being misunderstood. The up side of this, however, is that the more often we act, the quicker we are able to set the record straight.

Having read this chapter, one could easily conclude that there are so many different ways to be misunderstood, the only sure-fire way to avoid it is to avoid interaction itself. But that won't work either. After all, people could easily misunderstand why you were avoiding them. So there is really no point in becoming paranoid about it. Instead, we just have to realize that being misunderstood from time to time is inevitable. Of course, when that happens, it is normal to be concerned about it and to want to understand how it happened. It is also normal to want to blame it on someone else. If we understand how easily our actions can be misunderstood, however, we might be a bit more forgiving of ourselves, less inclined to blame others, and better able to avoid making the same mistakes again and again.

Notes

1. Unless otherwise indicated, all quotes appearing in this chapter are from *The 776 Stupidest Things Ever Said* (Petras and Petras 1993).

CHAPTER THREE

3 Observing

Behavior

Perception and

Misunderstanding

To perceive means to immobilize ... we seize, in the act of perception, something which outruns perception itself.

HENRI BERGSON, *French philosopher*

However, no two people see the world in exactly the same way. To every separate person a thing is what he thinks it is— in other words, not a thing, but a think.

PENELOPE FITZGERALD, *British author*

Like many other college professors, I am occasionally asked by local newspapers, radio, or television stations to comment on events that I might know something about. Like most people who talk to reporters, I do so with a certain amount of apprehension, as the result of having been misquoted in the past. Although I learned quite early in my career to be leery of newspaper interviews, for a while I naively assumed that a television interview would be less dangerous. After all, you can't be misquoted when you're there on the screen saying the words yourself. I quickly realized the error of this logic, however, when after my very first television interview key parts were edited out; the result was that I appeared to have said almost the exact opposite of what I had actually stated during the interview. I'm sure the news editor did not intentionally distort my message, but that is exactly what happened in the course of condensing a fifteen-minute interview into a two-minute sound bite. At the time, I was certain that if the entire interview had been telecast, no one would have misunderstood my intended message. I was wrong. Many of us watch the evening news in the midst of numerous distractions—dinner is being prepared, the children are asking about the dinner that is being prepared, the family pets are demanding that their dinner be prepared, other adults are talking about their day or asking about ours. In the midst of such distractions, we are unlikely to hear or pay attention to every word being broadcast on the tube. Under typical circumstances, many people would have missed part of and thus misunderstood my message even it had been broadcast in its entirety.

The problem is not unique to television viewing. At any moment in time there is just too much going on for us to possibly take it all in, and many misunderstandings are the result of this fundamental and unavoidable dilemma. Unlike video or tape recordings, human observation involves much more than a simple capturing of information. We not only gather information, we process it as we are gathering it. To make it even more complicated, during social interaction we do all this while simultaneously interacting with the people who are the sources of that information. At minimum, therefore, human observation involves two complex processes—perception and interpretation. Generally speaking, perception involves how and what we notice in our environment and interpretation involves how and what we think about the things we notice. Both processes are involved in formulating our understandings of each other.

I'll See It When I Believe It: The Influence of Expectation on Perception

At first blush, the title of this section appears to be a misquote or misstatement of the skeptic's aphorism *I'll believe it when I see it*. If so, it is a misstatement of which Freud would have been proud, for there is considerable scientific evidence that in a sense we see only what we already believe to exist. In fact, the primary theme of this chapter is that not only is seeing believing, but what is seen or heard sometimes depends on what is believed.

To see why this is, we need to understand something about how human perception works, for all understanding is rooted in perception. Unfortunately, perception is not simply a matter of opening our eyes and ears and taking in what is out there; it is an active process of selectively seeking out certain information. In fact, according to psychologist William Powers (1973), virtually all of our actions are geared toward controlling our perceptual experiences. If I perceive that it is starting to rain, I head for shelter. If I perceive an unexpected but familiar voice, I turn toward it. If I perceive that the hole I am digging is not yet deep enough, I keep digging, but if I perceive that my limbs are getting tired and weak, I dig more slowly or take a break from digging and sit down. If I perceive a hunger in my gut, I either move toward acquiring food or the purely mental action of talking to myself about waiting a while to eat. If I perceive that the person I am listening to is saying something I am interested in I listen more attentively, and depending on what I hear next, I'll keep listening carefully or allow my mind to wander to other things. My perceptions influence my actions and my actions influence what I perceive next. Thus, as Figure 1 shows, perception is an ongoing interaction between the individual and the environment in which the perceiver actively seeks out certain information from the environment and uses that information to direct further exploration (Neisser 1976). Because of the tremendous amount of sensory information available to us at any given moment, however, we have no choice but to selectively focus our attention on certain things at the expense of others.

The mental or cognitive structures that utilize perceptual information from prior experience to generate future expectations are referred to as "cognitive schemas." As we collect sensory information we process it in ways that are consistent with what we already know or believe to be true. When we encounter a similar situation in the future, particular cognitive schemas are triggered. These schemas allow us to anticipate certain events in the present situation, and our attention again will be guided by those anticipations or expectations. Thus, as shown in Figure 1, perception is an ever-evolving process in which the information to which our schemas direct our attention either reinforces the relevant schemas (if what we perceive is consistent with our expectations) or alters them if our perceptions are inconsistent with them. Thus precisely what we see when we look and what we hear when we listen depends on what we expect to see or hear. For example, although many people report having seen the "man in the moon," I have yet to find anyone who claims to have seen it before they were told that it was there and therefore were primed to look for it.

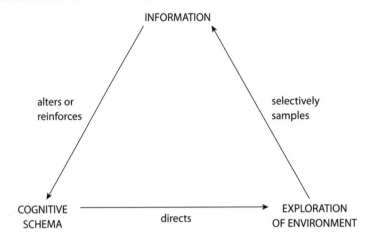

UNDERSTANDING

INFORMATION

alters or
reinforces

selectively
samples

COGNITIVE
SCHEMA

directs

EXPLORATION
OF ENVIRONMENT

Figure 1. *Model of the Perceptual Process (Adapted from Neisser 1976)*

Most perception is less consciously focused than the act of looking for the man in the moon, however. Once we have schemas for certain things, we do not have to consciously think about those things for the relevant schemas to be activated. For example, most of us can drive to work without getting lost or unconsciously running through any traffic signals, even if we are completely absorbed in thinking about something else. This is because we are familiar enough with the streets we travel to accurately anticipate traffic signals on certain corners, even if we are paying very little attention to our driving. In strange cities or unfamiliar parts of our own town, however, we don't know what to expect as we round each corner. Thus, even though we might be paying more attention there, we are more likely to cruise through an unnoticed red light.

Despite the powerful influence of expectations on what we are able to perceive, however, our schemas do not completely blind us to unexpected information. Although we will more easily notice things that are consistent with our expectations, we are certainly capable of eventually seeing or hearing things we don't expect, especially if those things are dramatically different from what we expect. We might not notice a fresh coat of paint on a friend's house, but we would notice if a new wing had been added. It is also possible to sense that something is not quite right without being able to identify precisely what is wrong, and sometimes we even see or hear things that aren't there.

Confusion of this sort is the result of a distortion of perception. Such distortions were the subject of a classic experiment conducted back in 1949 by Bruner and Postman. Using an instrument similar to the one an optometrist might use to test your vision, they presented subjects with very brief views of ordinary playing cards. Interspersed with the normal cards, however, were incongruous cards, such as red spades or black hearts. Initially subjects tended to identify the incongruous cards as normal, misidentifying either the color or the suit. Upon repeated exposure, however, many subjects began to notice that something wasn't right, but they tended to have what Bruner and Postman called "compromise reactions." Red spades were reported as brown, black and red mixed, or a number of other possible compromise colors and mixtures. As viewing time was increased accuracy was greatly enhanced, and when given enough time the subjects were eventually able to correctly identify the incongruous cards.

Given the highly selective nature of perception, it is easy to see how two people could experience the same event and come away with very different perceptions of what has occurred. This often happens when people are listening to music lyrics; although they are hearing the same song, they hear different words. In a humorous little book about this phenomenon, *'Scuse Me While I Kiss This Guy*, Gavin Edwards (1995) gives dozens of examples of commonly misheard lyrics. Not only do our ears seem to hear different things, our eyes often seem to see different things, even when we are witnessing the same event. Notice how often sports fans argue over whether a base runner is safe, a receiver is out of bounds when he catches a pass, or a collision on a basketball court, hockey rink, or soccer field is the result of a defensive or an offensive foul. Observers of feuding fans might reasonably wonder whether they have been watching the same game. Clearly, things are not always as they appear, and often we are poorly prepared to distinguish what really happens from what only appears to happen.

Social Perception: People and Situations

So far, this discussion has focused primarily on perception of the physical world, but you might already have realized that the perception of the social world of people and their actions works the same way. Just as the drive to work activates a schema that helps us navigate the physical world, so certain social cues activate schemas that are used to navigate the social world. Upon entering our places of work each morning, we are immediately prepared to hear the familiar greetings and see the familiar facial expressions of our co-workers. After a while our expectations of these daily rituals become so strongly entrenched that we probably would not even notice a casually stated "good evening" instead of "good morning."

I recently had a social experience analogous to the playing card experience of Bruner and Postman's (1949) subjects. I was at home anticipating a phone call from a friend. When the phone rang I answered and heard the expected voice on the other end. However, several seconds into the conversation I realized I was not talking to the person I had expected. Because I was anticipating one voice, I literally heard the voice on the phone differently from how I otherwise would have. Although I remember thinking the caller sounded a little different from usual, I did not initially perceive that I was actually talking to a different person.

Our expectations influence the way we perceive others in countless ways, and our expectations are often far from rational. In an interesting study of how irrational expectations influence perception, Mark Frank and Thomas Gilovich (1988) discovered that people tended to rate professional sports uniforms that were at least half black as being more "bad," "mean," and "aggressive" looking than others. When the experimenters showed the same aggressive football plays to a group of trained referees, the referees rated the plays as more deserving of a penalty when the aggressive players were clad in black than when they were dressed in white. These authors also noted that hockey and football teams that wear black have been penalized significantly more often than others. Thus it appears that even professional sports referees, who are selected on the basis of their ability to be objective, were influenced by the irrational, and no doubt unconscious, expectation that players wearing black would be overly aggressive in their play.

Just as we have schemas of people and things, so we have schemas of situations, which influence the way we perceive people and their actions in those situations. Situation schemas are activated by what sociologists call "definitions of the situation." Referring to situations by names such as "birthday parties" or "business meetings" activates schematic images that lead us to define those situations in particular ways. Those definitions include fairly specific expectations of (1) what kinds of actors will be present, (2) what kinds of actions they will be engaged in, and (3) how we will fit ourselves into the overall sequence of events. For example, we know that a birthday party usually involves three types of actors: the person whose birthday is celebrated, the person or persons who host the party, and those who attend. We also know that certain actions will be part of the situation. Food will be served and eaten, presents will be given and received, and a happy birthday song will be sung. With only slight variations, all these characteristics of the situation are defined by the culture we live in and will be present regardless of whose birthday is being celebrated or who attends the party. Such cultural expectations are only a part of the individual's definition of the situation, however, for each individual who attends will have his or her own personal orientation to the occasion. Some people like birthday parties, others do not; some see a party as a chance to relax and have fun, others as a chance to make new business contacts; some treat gift selection seriously and spend hours looking for just the right thing, others feel comfortable slipping a check or cash into a card.

Both cultural and personal definitions influence our expectations in all social situations, and these definitions enhance our perception of some things and limit our perception of others. The power of cultural definitions to limit our ability to perceive is illustrated by the following riddle.

> *A young boy and his father were out for a drive when they were involved in an automobile accident. An ambulance arrived quickly and took them to the hospital, where the father was pronounced dead and the son, who had sustained serious injuries, was rushed into surgery. Just before the surgery was to begin the surgeon looked down at the boy and exclaimed, "I can't operate on this boy; he's my son."*

How is this possible? Although the answer is revealed by the use of simple logic, many very intelligent people are at least momentarily stymied by it. As we listen to stories like this we develop a mental image of the situation being described and the actors involved. Because in our society the medical profession is dominated by males, the image of the male surgeon leads many of us to overlook the obvious fact that the surgeon in this story must be the boy's mother. Thus, our rather rigid schematic image of an operating room figures so prominently in our thinking that we overlook the obvious.

Once a situation schema is activated, the mental image that produces it is often so vivid and detailed that we assume we know exactly what to expect. As a result, we overlook or fail to pay attention to information that does not fit that image. The following misunderstanding is the type that often results from such a failure.

> *The last misunderstanding that occurred was about two months ago. I told my friend that I would pick him up from school on Friday. I have a white Buick and my sister has a gray Sentra. We decided to take one car home that weekend, and we took my sister's. When I went to pick up my friend, he never showed up. I finally went around the campus looking for him and found him. He asked if I was late because he couldn't find my car. I then realized that maybe he didn't know what my sister's car looked like and that is why he couldn't find it. He told me that I said I was going to be in my car, but I thought I said that I would pick him up in my sister's car. It was a misunderstanding because we were not clear on what car I was going to bring.*

There is no way of knowing who was at fault for this misunderstanding, but if it was a common occurrence for the narrator to use his car to give his friend a ride, the friend probably had a fairly vivid schema for that situation, which was activated as soon as the narrator agreed to pick him up (or perhaps even before the phone call was placed). If so, expecting his friend to say, "OK, I'll pick you up in my car," as he had in the past, he might easily have failed to hear the word "sister's."

Social situations are not always as predefined and ritualized as a birthday party or medical operation. Most are created spontaneously in the course of interaction, although once created they often take on a character of their own that influences our expectations of each other. You have probably at some time found yourself seated beside a stranger on a plane, bus, or train. One of you might have struck up a casual conversation with the other. Such conversations typically are characterized by superficial and lighthearted chatter about the weather, your destinations, or perhaps the reason you are traveling. If the conversation goes well, you might begin to sense the emergence of a rapport and mutual liking. When this happens, your expectations for what are appropriate and likely conversation topics begin to change. As the conversation drifts to more intimate topics, however, one or the other of you begins to disengage, and pretty soon you have both retreated into the safety of a book, magazine, or the passing scenery. What has happened? In all likelihood, at some point in the interaction your perceptions of the situation diverged, with one of you defining it as a conversation between intimates while the other still saw it as an interaction between relative strangers. A comment or action that would have been perfectly acceptable according to one perception was clearly unacceptable according to the other. If one party to an interaction perceives that he or she has crossed a threshold of intimacy while the other does not, the results can often be embarrassing. Thus the maintenance of a shared definition of the situation is as important as an accurate perception of the other person for maintaining mutual understanding and satisfactory interaction.

I Said–You Said: Actor–Observer Differences in Perception

Imagine that you have just bought a new car. The next day, while showing it to a friend, he asks you why you decided on this particular car. What would your answer sound like? In all likelihood your explanation would center on describing the characteristics of the car: its reliability, styling, roominess, gas mileage, cost, and so on. Although different people might stress different characteristics, most would nevertheless answer such a question by talking about the car. Now, suppose instead that your friend has just bought a new car and someone asks you your opinion about why he chose that particular vehicle. Your answer might be quite different. Rather than talking about the car, your reply would probably focus on your friend. "He's having a midlife crisis, so he decided to buy a sports car." "His wife just had another child, so they wanted something with lots of room." "He has a long commute, so he wanted something really reliable." In thinking about the causes of other people's actions, we tend to attribute their behavior to their unique needs, desires, or personality characteristics. In thinking about or explaining our own behavior, however, our emphasis typically centers on external factors. This difference reflects a fundamental contrast in the way actors and observers are oriented to the world. As actors, we are constantly having to adjust our actions to accommodate other people and the situations in which we find ourselves. As a result, when we think about why we have behaved in one way or another, we are inclined to focus on the situational or environmental conditions that influenced us, but as observers we tend to focus on whatever the actor is doing. This difference in focus leads us to attribute their actions to their own preferences or personal characteristics. It is not hard to see how actor–observer differences can lead to serious misunderstandings. Unless we force ourselves through conscious effort to mentally put ourselves in the position of the other and at least imagine how that person perceives the situation, we are unlikely to appreciate the external factors that influence his or her behavior.

Try to See Things My Way: Perceiving through the Eyes of the Other

Obviously, our ability to understand each other would be significantly enhanced if we could somehow temporarily switch positions with each other —if we could, as the old saying goes, walk a mile in each other's shoes. Although the 1988 movie *Trading Places,* starring Dan Ackroyd and Eddie Murphy, exploited this theme with considerable comedic success, it also showed quite dramatically just how different life can appear from the vantage point of another. Although such literal trading of places may be restricted to the world of fiction, we do have the ability to at least imagine how things must look from the perspective of the other, and as I have already indicated, our ability to achieve mutual understanding and satisfactory interaction depends largely on our ability to do just that.

Social psychologists use the term *role-taking* to describe this process. According to pioneering social psychologist George H. Mead (1934), role-taking involves mentally placing ourselves in the position of the other in order to see the world, including ourselves, from that person's perspective. Successful role-taking is necessary in order to formulate our own actions in a way that will be meaningful and acceptable to others. After carefully studying the development of role-taking abilities among adolescents, John Flavell (1968) suggested that it is an elaborate process requiring five interrelated steps. First, the individual must recognize the *existence* of other perspectives—that what we perceive, think, or feel in any given situation is not necessarily what others perceive, think, or feel. Although most people develop this understanding fairly early, it is amazing how often adults seem to forget it and assume that everyone else shares their view. Second, the individual must realize that taking the other's perspective would be useful in achieving a particular goal. One of the primary determinants of whether or not we perceive such a need is the extent to which the attainment of our goals depends on the cooperation of others. It is quite simply less necessary for one in a position of power to take into consideration the views of subordinates than for subordinates to understand the perspectives of those in positions of authority. Overt reminders of the value of role-taking, in some cases, may be sufficient to trigger such activity. Recognizing the need to take the role of the other, however, does not guarantee that the individual has the ability to effectively do so. Third, the person must be able to successfully carry out a role-taking analysis, which Flavell calls "prediction." In general, the ability to predict another person's reaction tends to improve as a result of maturation and repeated exposure to a diversity of others. Fourth, it is necessary to maintain a fix on the other person's perspective, especially if it contradicts one's own view of things. This step, which Flavell calls "maintenance," is especially difficult to accomplish if the perspective of the other is radically different from one's own. Whenever people say, "I can see your point, but . . . ," they are probably having difficulty with maintenance. Finally, role-taking is of little use if we cannot apply the insights gained from it to the situation at hand. Thus Flavell's final stage—the *application* stage—is where we again assume the role of actor in formulating a response to the actions of the other.

The first four stages in this process (existence, need, prediction, and maintenance) are necessary in order to understand the actions of the other from that person's perspective, and the final stage (application) is necessary if our response is to be accurately understood by the other. As a result of failures in role-taking, conflicts sometimes reach the point where both parties have acted in ways the other considers rude, inappropriate, or insensitive. Overcoming such impasses can be facilitated by forcing each party to view the situation from the point of view of the other. Perhaps the easiest way to accomplish this from within the situation is to calmly ask the person with whom you are in conflict to explain how he or she thinks it all got started, explaining that you want to try to see it from his or her perspective. Listen carefully to what the person says and, when he or she is finished, offer to explain how you perceived things. If both are willing not only to listen, but also to empathize with the other, the chances of reconciliation will be greatly enhanced.

Conclusion: Why Looking Is Not Necessarily Seeing

This chapter has focused primarily on the problematic nature of human, especially social, perception. Due to certain limitations that we have as biological beings, it is impossible to truly observe all that our immediate environment makes available to us at any given moment. Thus perception is highly selective. We are less likely to see what we don't expect to see because we are not looking for it. Some unexpected events are sufficiently dramatic to force their way into our span of attention, but many of the more subtle aspects of human action will be missed to the extent that we do not expect them. Moreover, our expectations are often influenced by such biasing factors as cultural stereotypes and personal experiences that, although very salient to us, are not at all typical or consistent with the experiences of others.

Americans place a great value on personal experience. As a teacher of criminology, I am frequently confronted by students whose real-world experiences seem to be contradicted by the results of research findings I present in class. When confronted with such contradictions, the inclination of many people is to deny the validity of the research in favor of their own experience. Such an attitude, while understandable, misses two important points. First, it assumes that their experiences are typical, that the experiences of other people in other places are the same as their own. This assumption is often easily refuted by simply bringing other people into the conversation. The police officer, for example, who says, based on his experience, that intervention in domestic abuse cases has no effect on offenders is likely to be challenged by another police officer who cites cases of her own that do show an effect. The more we learn about the experiences of others who are different from ourselves, the less we are inclined to assume that our experiences and perceptions are shared by everyone else.

The second and somewhat more subtle point is that we often fail to recognize that we are participants in the world we observe, and as such we influence events in ways we might not realize. For example, research on police confrontations with juveniles reveals that the probability of an arrest taking place depends in part on the demeanor displayed by juveniles in their interactions with officers. Holding other factors constant, kids who react to questioning by the police with what the officers consider the proper respect are less likely to be arrested. What the arresting officers fail to realize in some cases is that the youths' demeanor is influenced by the way in which they are approached by the police and by the experiences they have had with other police officers. Thus officers who expect certain youths to be confrontational might be inclined to display an overtly tough posture in order to seize initial control of the situation. With some juveniles, this approach serves to create the very problem it is intended to circumvent. In short, we are usually not passive observers of the world; we are participant observers, and thus we play an active role in creating the events we observe.

Our perception of events is affected not only by the expectations we have of the people involved, but also by our expectations of what actions are typical and thus should occur in particular situations. Our definition of the situation will influence what we expect to occur and will thus direct our attention toward those types of events and away from others. Expecting the glass to be half full leads us to focus on the water; expecting it to be half empty leads us to focus on the space above the water.

Another limitation on our ability to perceive events in their full complexity is that we can only see things from our own unique physical and social vantage point. For example, observers are naturally inclined to focus on the actions of the actor, whereas actors are inclined to focus their attention on those forces in the immediate environment to which they must respond and which they must take into account in formulating their actions. Moreover, inasmuch as normal interaction involves our continually switching back and forth between the role of observer and that of actor, we must pay close attention to the actions of the other in order to act in ways that are situationally appropriate. This makes it even more difficult for us to take the time to imagine how the interaction must appear to the other. Unfortunately, effective interaction requires that we do so. Developing our skills as role-takers is one of the few means at our disposal for counteracting the selective and often biased view we have of our interactions with others. If there is one skill that is likely to enhance our success as interactants, it is the ability to successfully see the world from the perspective of the other. Therefore, this chapter concludes with a role-taking exercise.

ROLE-TAKING EXERCISE

The next time you find yourself unable to understand the behavior of another person, try working through the following steps in the role-taking process.

1. **Existence** *Does the other person have a different definition of the situation from mine? (The answer is very likely to be "yes" if the two of you occupy different social positions, especially if one of you has more power than the other—for example, in an employer–employee relationship.)*
2. **Need** *Would I benefit from being able to see the situation as the other sees it? If so, how?*
3. **Prediction** *Try to imagine that you are the other; imagine the pressures (social, emotional, financial, etc.) and influences that might affect that person's viewpoint. Imagine how you might act under those same pressures and influences.*
4. **Maintenance** *If you have been successful so far, you should have a bit more understanding of the other's behavior. At this point, however, the tendency is to think, "OK, maybe I can see why he acted that way, but that is no excuse." If so, you are slipping out of the role of the other and back into your own view. Remember, you are not trying to find excuses for the other, you are just trying to understand him or her, for your own benefit.*

5. **Application** *If you truly understand the other better, how can you use that understanding to repair the damage that has been done and avoid such misunderstandings in the future?*

Hint: If you decide to share with the other your newfound understanding of his or her behavior, be careful to avoid sounding condescending. Remember, actions speak louder than words.

CHAPTER

FOUR

4

Making Sense

of What We

Perceive

The Problem

of Interpretation

Sir, I have found you an argument;
but I am not obliged to find you an
understanding.

SAMUEL JOHNSON, *British author*

Poetry is what is lost in translation.

ROBERT FROST, *American poet*

Although accurate perception is necessary, it does not guarantee un-derstanding, which is achieved only through a complex process of interpretation. It is only through interpretation that we are able to make sense of or give meaning to what we perceive. No doubt you have had experiences like the following. While working in my study one evening I noticed a tapping noise. At first I paid little attention to it, but as it persisted I began to try to figure out the source of the noise. Knowing that I was home alone, my first guess was that one of my neighbors was hammering something. But then I realized that my neighbors on both sides were out of town and anyhow the noise was too loud and clear to be coming from that far away. I thus concluded that the sound was coming from my own property. As I listened more attentively, I also realized that the tapping was much too rapid to be the work of human hands. Perhaps telephone or power company workers were working in front of my house, but why would they be working so late and making so much noise? My curiosity finally got the better of me and I walked outside to investigate. As soon as I opened the door, the noise stopped and I realized there was no one near the house. I gently closed the door and listened again. After a moment the tapping returned. I finally realized that the sound was coming from the other side of the house. Walking to that side and looking out a window, I saw the darkened figure of a woodpecker hammering away at one of my oak trees. I went out and requested that he leave, he obliged, and I returned to work.

A number of activities common to interpretation are present in this little story, but for now let me point out just a couple. First, notice that in order to interpret the sound, I was forced to actively collect additional sensory information. Not only did I have to take a second listen, I eventually had to follow the sound in order to take a look. As the model of perception discussed previously would predict, each action was based on previous perceptions. Second, as soon as I began trying to make sense of the noise, I became consumed by one of the most common forms of interpretive activity—trying to understand the source or cause of the perceived event. Social psychologists refer to this as the "attribution process." Third, the attribution process involved in this simple act of interpretation was restricted to trying to understand what was causing the noise, for as soon as I realized that the tapping had been the work of a woodpecker, my curiosity was satisfied. I didn't ask myself or the perpetrator why he was pecking away at one of my trees, for I already knew the answer. That's just what he does!

Would the story have ended where it did had I discovered the source of the noise to have been a person? Say, for example, it had turned out to have been my neighbor using a chisel to remove tiles from her patio. I would have begun immediately to ask myself questions that I did not ask about the woodpecker. Why did my neighbor return early from her trip? Why was she removing tiles from her patio? Why was she doing it so late at night? When it comes to interpreting the actions of people, we are not satisfied simply to know what they are doing or even what their purposes are. We also want to know their motives. After all, people don't just do things, they do them for reasons. This means that in order to understand people we need to make sense of three things: (1) actions (What are they doing?), (2) purposes (What is the goal behind their action?), and (3) motives (Why are they pursuing that particular goal?). Once we have identified what they are doing, the purpose behind the action is usually pretty clear. If someone smiles and extends a hand as you approach, it is almost certainly in order to issue a greeting. But why does that person wish to greet you? Is it because she likes you, because she wants something from you, or simply because she sees it as a social obligation? Motives are more difficult to assess, but we give them a high priority because we assume they reveal something important about the individual. Understanding the causes or motives behind people's actions, therefore, is one of the most important and difficult forms of interpersonal understanding.

The process of interpreting causes and imputing motives is significantly more complex than the comparatively simple perception of action, primarily because the same action can have very different meanings, depending on the social context. I will take up this topic in more detail in a later chapter, but for now consider the complexity of interpreting the meaning of a simple raised hand. In various social contexts, the same gesture may be interpreted as (1) a signal for traffic to stop, (2) a Nazi salute, (3) an attempt to get someone's attention, (4) a signal that a student knows the answer to a question, or (5) a gesture of greeting. Because of this complexity, many misunderstandings result from the errors we make in interpreting what we perceive.

The complexity of interpreting human actions requires that we often use what psychologists call "judgment heuristics." These are essentially rules or strategies we employ to simplify the task of interpretation. These interpretive shortcuts allow us to make quick and easy interpretations on the basis of relatively little information. One of the most commonly employed judgment heuristics is the *representative heuristic,* which is simply the idea that the more closely individuals resemble members of a certain category, the more likely they are to act like members of that category. For example, if a man drives a pickup truck, wears cowboy boots, and sports a short haircut he is likely to be seen as an example of a particular social type. Once we have classified him as that type, we expect him to have certain other characteristics. For example, we might guess that he resides in the South or West, drinks lots of beer, and thinks that flag burners and drug dealers should be given the death penalty. Although we might be wrong in each of these assumptions, we would be inclined to interpret his behavior according to such beliefs. Several years ago I met a person who fit that description pretty closely. He turned out to be a campus radical from upstate New York who sold illegal drugs. He contended that, because of his appearance, he had never been suspected of illegal activities by university authorities or the police, despite the fact that he had actively used and sold drugs for years.

Another commonly employed heuristic is the *attitude heuristic*. Attitudes are essentially the overall positive or negative feelings we have about people and things and are usually expressed in such terms as *like* or *dislike, for* or *against.* Attitudes not only express our feelings about things but also influence how we interpret events related to those things. For example, Tom and Bill have very different attitudes toward President Clinton. Tom likes him and Bill dislikes him. These attitudes influence their interpretations of practically everything Clinton does. On the rare occasion that the president proposes legislation that Bill favors, Bill interprets it as a ploy on the part of the president to get reelected, and on the rare occasion that he proposes legislation that Tom does not support, Tom interprets it as a necessary compromise with an unreasonable Congress. Like all heuristics, attitudes simplify the complex task of social perception by providing us with a consistent perspective from which to view and interpret the actions of others, but they also inhibit our ability to objectively perceive and evaluate information. Thus they bias our understanding of people and their actions in various ways. In the next section I will consider some of the more common biases that characterize the interpretive process.

Attribution Biases: Why It's So Hard to Be Objective

In Chapter 3, I suggested that, because of their mutually exclusive perspectives, actors and observers cannot be expected to see things exactly the same way. Both are somewhat biased as a result of their inability to see things from the point of view of the other. This *actor–observer bias* poses obvious problems for maintaining mutual understanding. However, even if we were able to somehow overcome this bias, we would still find ourselves frequently at odds with others because of basic differences in the way we interpret events. The process of using various social cues to interpret the meaning and causes of behavior is referred to as the "attribution process." Like perceptual errors, attribution errors are usually not random but are the result of systematic biases in the way we interpret the actions of others. Let us briefly consider some of the more important and well documented of such biases.

Ignoring the Situation: The Fundamental Attribution Bias

For most of us, life is full of ups and downs, and regardless of which direction it seems to be headed at any moment, we are likely to assume that it is the direct result of human action. If friends or relatives forget our birthday, we might accuse them of being self-centered and inconsiderate. But, if they buy us nice presents or take us out for a fun celebration, we assume it is because they are thoughtful and loving. When things don't go as we want or expect them to go, we are quick to assume that someone is at fault, and when things go well, we are almost as quick to find someone to thank. Although it is often more appropriate to blame circumstances than individuals, we humans—especially those of us raised in societies that stress individualism and free will—show a persistent preference for blaming, as well as crediting, people instead of social circumstances. The tendency to make personal or internal attributions rather than situational or external attributions in explaining both positive and negative outcomes is what psychologist Lee Ross has termed the "fundamental attribution bias." What makes this tendency a bias is not simply that we more often make personal or internal rather than situational or external attributions, but that we tend to do so even when the facts clearly do not support such an interpretation.

As a test of the fundamental attribution error, Ross, Amabile, and Steinmetz (1977) devised a simulated TV quiz show in which they randomly assigned subjects to be either "quiz masters" or "contestants." Quiz masters were told to think up ten difficult questions for the contestants to try to answer. Contestants were able to correctly answer an average of only four out of ten questions. Observers of the simulation were aware that the assignment of subjects as either quiz masters or contestants had been based purely on chance, and thus there was no reason to believe the quiz masters to be smarter or more knowledgeable than those chosen to be contestants. Moreover, general knowledge tests given to the participants revealed that contestants and quiz masters were equally knowledgeable. Nevertheless, after viewing the simulation, observers rated the quiz masters as being significantly more knowledgeable than the contestants, overlooking the obvious advantage of the quiz masters and the difficulty of the task faced by the contestants. Notice that I did not say that observers of the simulated quiz show rated the contestants as abnormally ignorant; the primary bias was in the tendency to perceive the quiz masters as exceptionally knowledgeable. Thus the fundamental attribution error influences our interpretation of positive as well as negative performances. Not only are we more likely to conclude that people who behave badly do so because they have negative personal characteristics, we are also inclined—perhaps even more strongly—to believe that behavior we approve of is the result of the good or admirable personal characteristics of actors.

Why are we prone to give disproportionate weight to the internal dispositions of actors instead of recognizing the myriad situational factors that influence behavior? Due in large part to the actor–observer difference described earlier, when we observe a social setting our attention naturally is focused on the actions of other actors in the situation. Because we occupy a different perceptual vantage point, we are often unaware of the various factors actors take into consideration in formulating their behavior. Thus we are not likely to see such factors as important causes of their behavior. To the extent that we do not or cannot consider the situational factors that influence behavior, we are certain to frequently misunderstand why others do the things they do.

According to social psychologist Mark Snyder (1974), individuals differ in how closely they monitor the behavior of others for cues to appropriate behavior. He refers to high self-monitors as those who closely monitor their own actions and the actions of those around them in order to formulate actions that are appropriate to the situation. Low self-monitors, on the other hand, scrutinize the actions of others less closely because they are primarily concerned that their own behavior reflect their true inner selves, with less regard to what might be considered situationally appropriate. Because they are more attuned to the demands of the situation, high self-monitors should be less likely to commit the fundamental attribution error. However, neither style is without its problems, as the following student account reveals.

> My best friend and I are both introverts. We spent the first six years of our education in a small private school, where the social situation as well as the behaviors and attitudes were fairly consistent. The amount of self-monitoring in order to be able to fit in with the other students was at a minimum. We had gone to a school with those same students since the first grade. But after sixth grade, my best friend and I moved to a public middle school. We did not know anyone, nor did we understand their system of classes. We were forced to do some self-monitoring in order to know how to behave and present ourselves in public school ... I was able to watch the other students who seemed to be popular and well liked by other students and teachers. I was able to present myself in that same manner and found that I adapted fairly well to the new situation of public school, even though I was not presenting my true self to others. I behaved in a way to match everyone else. My friend saw these same students, but was unable to change her behavior to meet the needs of the new situation. She was consistent in her introverted behavior across situations and was met many times with ridicule from the other students. She did not act or behave the same way they did so therefore they rejected her ... High self-monitoring can be a highly useful ability, but at the same time it can cause its own problems. High self-

monitors can be seen as manipulative or insincere. In my case though, because of my introverted nature, I found myself becoming completely exhausted from school. The constant need to match others' behaviors while inside wanting to be quiet and alone caused great stress. I began to realize that no one knew the real me. My friend was able to find her own small niche in the school. She did not have the same turmoil of trying to act like a completely different person. She put her true self out there, and people could either like it or not. After reaching a final crisis in my constant high self-monitoring, I have attempted to become more like my friend. I try to still be adaptable in my behavior, but when I begin to feel uncomfortable or feel that I have strayed too far away from my real self, I have learned how to lower my self-monitoring.

Because of the sometimes dramatic difference in their orientations to the social environment, high and low self-monitors are probably frequently inclined to misunderstand each other's motives. A popular interpretation of the behaviors of high self-monitors is that they are insincere, that they give others what they want in order to get what they want from others. This ignores the fact that high self-monitors provide a service to those around them. By accommodating their behavior to the situational expectations of others, they make others feel comfortable and facilitate interaction. On the other hand, low self-monitors are often criticized for being uncompromising and frequently inappropriate. But this criticism ignores the fact that low self-monitors provide the service of putting a check on overconformity, thus providing others who might not always want to go along with the crowd with role models for resisting social pressure. Clearly, these two styles complement each other in many ways. Just imagine a world in which everyone was a high self-monitor. Now imagine one in which everyone was a low self-monitor. Most of us would prefer the world we have, where both styles coexist, with each providing a balance to the other, and where most people fall somewhere between these two extremes. Are you a high or low self-monitor? To find out, take the self-monitoring test presented at the end of this chapter.

Taking Credit and Shifting Blame: The Self-Serving Bias

As actors, we are naturally focused on the situational factors that influence our behavior, but that does not mean that we always attribute the outcomes of our actions to situational forces. In fact, there is a pervasive tendency for actors to willingly accept personal responsibility when things go right but deny responsibility when things go wrong. Thus, when outcomes are assessed in terms of success or failure, our interpretations are often influenced by a *self-serving bias*. This seems to be the result of a basic need we all have to maintain a positive self-concept. Unlike the actor–observer

UNDERSTANDING

bias, which is based on the way we perceive events, the self-serving bias is based on the way we interpret events. Moreover, the self-serving bias is often strong enough to reverse the conclusions suggested by the actor–observer bias. That is, as a result of the actor–observer bias, we should be inclined to always attribute the causes of our own acts to environmental factors and the causes of others' acts to personal factors. However, the need to have events reflect well on us often leads us to attribute our successful actions to our own personal characteristics or efforts. Likewise, whenever we take credit for the successes of others, we defy the actor–observer bias by attributing their success to something in their environment (i.e., ourselves) rather than something within them.

The self-serving bias can be seen frequently in work settings. When students come to talk to me about bad grades they have received on tests or papers, they typically report having studied for their exam or worked on their paper long and hard and of being surprised and disappointed that their grade was so low. Although they usually don't come right out and say it, there is often the implication that they didn't do well because the test was too hard or my grading too rigorous. Alternative explanations often involve references to such external causes as illness, stress, emotional problems, or other mitigating factors over which they had no control. Because such explanations are consistent with actors' tendencies to focus on situational factors, they cannot necessarily be attributed to the self-serving bias. However, the self-serving bias is reflected in the fact that they never attribute their high grades to such situational factors as easy questions, lenient grading, or good teaching. Instead, good grades are attributed to hard work and ability. I must confess, however, that often I fall into the same trap. When grades are low, I tend to become discouraged about the motivation and level of preparation of my students or the long hours many of them devote to things other than school work, convinced that my tests are reasonable and my grading standards appropriate. Again, however, these interpretations are consistent with my position as an observer of their performance. When grades are high, the self-serving bias allows me to feel proud of what a good job of teaching I have done. Thus, initially at least, both the students and I are influenced by the self-serving bias as we attempt to take credit for good grades.

Our tendency to employ the self-serving bias often puts us at odds with others. The following is an unedited account provided by one of my former students.

Early Tuesday morning during Mardi Gras in Fat City, I was walking with a friend down a street. This nice looking girl walked by and I said, "Hey Baby, how are you doing." She didn't say anything so I told my friend that she acted like a bitch. She must have heard what I said, she started cursing me and trying to hit me with a bottle. I tried to calm her down, but that didn't work. I got tired of her trying to hit me with that longneck, so I told her that I'd never hit a girl before, but if she hit me with that bottle I would knock her ass out. This would be a misunderstanding because I didn't call her a bitch, I said she was acting like a bitch. She was the one being unsociable, not me.

Notice how this student exhibits the self-serving bias in this account. First, he demonstrates the observer bias by interpreting her initial nonresponse as a snub and attributing it to a personal characteristic. Ultimately he succumbs to the self-serving bias, however, as he attributes the altercation to a misunderstanding rather than to his having referred to her as a bitch. As he put it, "She was the one being unsociable, not me."

Although the self-serving bias often leads to interpersonal conflict, it is not an altogether bad tendency, for by allowing us to protect our self-esteem it gives us the courage to persist despite occasional setbacks. Research by William Schaufeli (1988), for example, revealed that unemployed workers who exhibited the self-serving bias were more successful at finding new employment than those who were more objective about their situation. Thus, research suggests that the individual who does not occasionally employ this bias is more likely to suffer low self-esteem and, as a result, may be less likely to succeed.

Our Team Never Cheats: The Ultimate Attribution Error

Biased attributions are not restricted to those that benefit ourselves. Parents are notorious for overlooking the faults of their offspring, but all of us are inclined to make attributions that benefit those with whom we identify. Suppose you are informed that your best friend has just failed to get a job promotion she had been hoping for. Instead, the promotion was given to someone you distinctly dislike. This situation can be explained in two possible ways: either your friend didn't deserve the promotion as much as the other person, or the decision to deny your friend the promotion was unjust. Unless you are unusually objective, you are likely to believe the explanation that favors your friend.

I live in the Dallas–Fort Worth area, so most of the people I know are Dallas Cowboys fans, even those who don't particularly care about football. In 1994 the Cowboys lost in the National Football Conference championship game to the San Francisco Forty-Niners, who went on to win the Super Bowl that season. Deion Sanders, then a defensive back for the Forty-Niners, was instrumental in the San Francisco victory. Not surprisingly, after that game Sanders was vilified by Texas sportswriters and Dallas fans. Prior to the beginning of the 1995 season, however, Deion left the Forty-Niners and became a member of the Cowboys team. One year and one Dallas Super Bowl victory later Deion Sanders was one of the most popular sports figures in the state of Texas. In 1994 Sanders was seen by Dallas fans as an overrated hot dog; in 1995 he was considered by those same fans to be one of the most exciting players and all around nice guys in the game.

Both of these examples point to another type of bias in the way we interpret events—one that social psychologist Thomas Pettigrew (1979) refers to as the "ultimate attribution bias." The *ultimate attribution bias* refers to our tendency to make attributions that favor those we perceive to be within our group and disfavor those outside our group. Pettigrew initially identified this tendency in his study of ethnic and racial prejudice. Since then, however, researchers have shown that it works in a variety of contexts. In my own research on perceptions of crime and the criminal justice system, for example, I have found that Anglo Americans are much more likely than African Americans to perceive police and judges, most of whom are white, to be fair and unbiased in their dealings with citizens.

While most of us are willing to admit that we probably do commit the ultimate attribution error on occasion, we nevertheless tend to see each of our individual interpretations as essentially valid. Thus, although we are willing to admit that we are cognitive sinners, we are inclined to deny each of our individual sins. Why? Why do we find it so difficult to admit that we are biased in this way? On the basis of my experiences with thousands of college students, I have found that when pushed to the limits of their ability to rationalize, people will admit their biases. However, as creatures who value both morality and rationality, we are inclined to believe that we should think rationally and act morally. Since it is generally considered both irrational and unfair to be consciously prejudiced or biased in our assessments of others, we are motivated to maintain some degree of consistency between our beliefs about people and our feelings about them. For example, if I have positive feelings about Paul and negative feelings about Nathan, and I observe an event that casts a positive light on Nathan and a negative light on Paul, how am I to make sense of this? As in the example of the friend being deprived of a job promotion, I have only two basic choices. Either I can conclude that I was wrong in my assessments of these two people, or I can construct an explanation that rationally explains the unexpected event and at the same time allows me to maintain my original attitudes toward them. Because of the ultimate attribution bias, I am most likely to opt for the latter. After all, imagine how confusing and exhausting life would be if we had to change our basic beliefs and feelings toward people every time their behavior disappointed us. Besides, likes and dislikes are not always rational, and it is often impossible to change the way we feel about people no matter how unjustified those feelings seem.

But this raises another question. Why can't we just accept the fact that people we like occasionally act in ways we don't like and that people we don't like occasionally act in ways we like? Obviously we can and sometimes do, but if that happened very often, eventually we would have to wonder whether our preferences were at all justified. Thus, the ultimate attribution bias protects our personal relationships and group identifications while at the same time it helps us maintain the sense that we are being rational, even when we are not!

Personal Consequences of Attributional Style

Our inclination to blame or credit people, including ourselves, depends on whether we make internal or external attributions, and as we have already seen, our attributions are often quite biased. Although the internal–external dimension of attributions is important, other dimensions are also important in determining how we make sense of events. For example, imagine that you have an argument with a co-worker and are trying to understand your role in the conflict and what it means for the future of your relationship. One question you are likely to seriously ponder is whether the altercation was your fault (internal attribution) or not (external attribution), and the way you feel about yourself will be influenced significantly by the attribution you make. Let's assume that you conclude that the argument was largely your fault. That is not likely to make you feel very good about yourself. On the other hand, you might find it easier to forgive yourself if you conclude that it was a rare event, that you normally get along well with others and do not often do things that cause conflict. That is, causing conflict with others is not a stable personal characteristic; perhaps you were just having a bad day. Your feelings about yourself would be considerably more negative, however, if you realized that this incident was part of a larger pattern of frequent conflicts with others, perhaps reflecting a fixed personality trait. Thus, events may be the result of either internal or external causes, and they may reflect either stable personality traits or temporary psychological states.

There is yet a third dimension of attributions that influences how we feel about ourselves and others, and that is whether or not the observed outcome appears to be restricted to a particular type of situation. For example, suppose you often find yourself in conflict with others, but that it only seems to happen when you are under a great deal of stress at work. While it might be disappointing to realize that you become overly aggressive under pressure, that would be preferable to knowing that you act that way in all kinds of situations.

Whenever we attribute negative events to internal, stable, and global causes, there is every reason to expect that such negative events will occur again and again in the future, and that is a pretty bleak prospect. According to Paul Sweeney, Karen Anderson, and Scott Bailey (1986), who reviewed over one hundred studies on attributional style, individuals who are more likely than others to attribute negative events to internal, stable, and global causes also are more inclined than others to attribute positive outcomes to external, unstable, and specific causes. That is, those who attribute their failures to personal deficiencies are also inclined to attribute their successes to luck. More importantly, a *depressive attributional style* has been linked to higher levels of psychological depression and physical illness than the more *optimistic style* of those who attribute their failures to bad luck and their success to personal competence.

In our society women more often suffer depression than men. Given this fact, it is not surprising that research has shown that girls are more likely than boys to have a depressive attributional style. When good things happen to girls, many of them are inclined to attribute it to luck, but when bad things happen they are inclined to blame themselves. Boys, on the other hand, are more likely to attribute their successes to ability and their failures to bad luck or other factors outside their control. I will discuss other dimensions of this difference in more detail in the chapter on gender and misunderstanding. For now, however, it is important to recognize that the kinds of attributions we make in interpreting events will not only influence how we understand and relate to others and how we feel about ourselves, but also how we feel about life in general. According to psychologist Lyn Abramson and colleagues (1978), our understanding of the relationship between attributional style and depression has led to the development of certain cognitive therapies that in many cases have been more effective in the treatment of depression than the use of mood-altering drugs.

Although attribution style may in some cases cause depression, it also can be caused by a preexisting state of depression. That is, the generally negative and dismal view of life that comes with depression might lead one to adopt a depressive attributional style. However, regardless of which is the cause and which the effect, by altering the kinds of attributions we make we may be able to alter our overall sense of well-being.

It is important to recognize that all aspects of a depressive attributional style are not necessarily negative for the individual and that all aspects of an optimistic style are not necessarily positive. For example, the inclination to deny personal responsibility for negative events might make it easier to maintain an optimistic attitude, but it can also lead one to employ the self-serving bias and unfairly blame others for problems. If we are unable to acknowledge our deficiencies, we are unlikely to be able to overcome them. Moreover, a tendency to accept personal responsibility often makes it easier to get along with others, who are spared the anguish and embarrassment of having to admit their own culpability. Thus personal psychological discord and interpersonal discord are often opposite sides of the same attributional coin.

We all go through periods of depression, and during these periods we are apt to adopt a depressive attribution style. As a result we will often misunderstand the actions and intentions of others. For example, when depressed, we are more prone to feel unliked and unloved, partly because we misinterpret the actions of others. Regardless of how we might feel during a bout of depression, however, the fact that our friends haven't called us much recently does not mean that they no longer care for us. Likewise, our setbacks at work are not necessarily an indication of incompetence on our part. Understanding such things might be easy most of the time, but during periods of depression, logical thinking is hard to maintain. In order to help ourselves and others through occasional bouts of depression, therefore, we must take steps to break the cycle of negative attributions and depressive feelings. Recognizing the link between such negative thinking and feelings of hopelessness is the first step in this process.

The Sounds of Silence

This morning I walked into my 10:00 class at 10:02. The room was abuzz with the conversations of dozens of students. I stepped behind the podium, unloaded a stack of graded exams to be returned, and opened my notes as they continued to talk. Once organized, I stood silently gazing at them; within ten to twenty seconds the room was silent. I began my lecture. Silence communicates.

Although attribution frequently involves the interpretation of the meaning of utterances, often we are required to attribute meaning to the absence of talk. In many situations, it is as important to understand the meaning of silence as it is to understand the meaning of the words that border it. As Ivan Illich (1970:45) wrote in *Celebration of Awareness,* "The learning of a language is more the learning of its silences than of its sounds." There are tense moments when silence can be deafening, occasions when it can speak volumes, and situations in which it can communicate more eloquently than any words. Yet, as Illich points out, learning to decipher the grammar of silence is not an easy job. The task is especially daunting when we are dealing with a culture that is foreign to us, but the grammar is no less complex and capable of being misunderstood when the language is that of our own culture.

When silence is observed among adults in American society, it is typically perceived negatively. Silence may be assumed to indicate anger, as expressed by the declaration, "They're not talking." The aphorism "If you can't say something nice, don't say anything at all" suggests that silence will often be interpreted as an indication of disapproval. Prolonged periods of silence among intimates is frequently perceived as an indication of concern or worry: "You're so quiet; is something wrong?" Silence is also used as a metaphor for apathy, as in "the world stood by silently while Hitler butchered millions of Jews," or as a euphemism for lying, such as when the gangster advises the witnesses to his crime to "keep silent about this if you know what's good for you." Clearly implied in this admonition is that the witnesses are not only to keep silent about it if possible, but to lie about it if pressed by the authorities. Finally, in the American criminal justice system silence is often associated with guilt. The Fifth Amendment to the Constitution states that no person "shall be compelled in any criminal case to be a witness against himself." This right is most often observed in court by refusing to answer certain questions that might be self-incriminating. Unfortunately, in the context of American society such silence is often interpreted as a sign of guilt, as supported by the popular notion that an innocent person has nothing to hide. This of course ignores the possibility that certain conditions might operate to make an innocent person look guilty.

This is not to deny that silence can have positive connotations in certain situations. However, it is significant that, with the exception of libraries and classrooms during examinations—places where most Americans spend little time—silence is primarily valued where talk would interfere with the ability of others to *hear* something or someone else (for example, in church, theaters, concert halls, or while someone else is talking). If silence is golden, one can only assume that sound is platinum.

Despite the cultural preference for sound over silence, it is important for the interactant who would avoid misunderstanding to know when silence will be considered appropriate and when it will be considered inappropriate. Although social scientists have devoted relatively little attention to the identification of cultural norms regarding silence, it is clear that rules specifying where, when, and for whom silence is appropriate do exist. Among the most important determinants of silence norms is the social setting. For example, silence is routinely observed in such places as libraries, museums, churches, theaters, and funeral homes. Silence is also a part of various rituals, both religious and secular, the moment of silent reflection or prayer having been institutionalized in both types of settings.

There are also specific times during interaction when silence is considered appropriate and is expected, and there are times when it is likely to be awkward. For example, silence is normally not used to initiate interaction. If we want to engage someone in a conversation, we typically employ an opening line to which we can reasonably expect a reply. After all, silence toward someone who has just initiated a verbal interaction is considered rude. There are times, however, when silence is an appropriate tool for the initiation of interaction. Imagine that you need to talk to a co-worker who is busy working at her desk. If she appears to be in the middle of a task that requires a fair amount of concentration, there is an informal norm that you don't disturb her until she appears to be at a convenient stopping point. Since it may be difficult for you to know when she has reached that point, however, you may choose to use silence as a way of engaging her. Simply by walking up and standing silently by or in front of her desk until she acknowledges your presence, you are able to communicate that you wish to speak with her. Your silent presence says that you would like to talk but also that you are polite enough not to interrupt her until it is convenient for her. Likewise, the silent gesture of raising one's hand in a classroom or other formal group discussion setting is an appropriate way to initiate interaction.

Silence is also routinely observed at certain points during interaction. Perhaps the most frequently observed norm of silence in our culture is remaining silent while someone else is talking. A closely related norm is that of taking turns at talk. Those who interject comments while another is talking or still has the floor will be seen as aggressive and obnoxious. The problem, however, is that different groups conduct conversations at different paces. Deborah Tannen's (1985) research suggests that New York City Jews, for example, tend to talk relatively fast and allow shorter time to expire between turns than do "mainstream" American speakers. On the other extreme, the slow-talking Southerner is almost a cultural cliche. In normal conversation, speakers do not announce when they are finished talking and are prepared to allow someone else a turn. Interactants are thus required to interpret silent pauses and make judgments about when a pause does and when it does not indicate that the speaker is finished talking. Those accustomed to fast talking are thus more likely to take their turn before slow talkers are finished, while slow talkers will often miss opportunities to speak by allowing too long a silence before concluding that the fast talker is finished. Misunderstandings can result from such differences in speech patterns, with slower talkers perceiving faster talkers as rude and faster talkers sometimes perceiving slower talkers as shy, uninformed, or unsociable.

Another context in which delays in turn taking can be problematic is the question–answer format. Those who hesitate too long before answering a question run the risk of being perceived as less honest and straightforward than the faster respondent. The tendency to equate long response intervals with lying is suggested by the research of Anne Griffam Walker, who found that lawyers tend to presume dishonesty on the part of witnesses who hesitate before answering questions. Walker (1985) finds this tendency especially interesting in light of the fact that the leading textbooks on trial law teach lawyers to advise their own witnesses to think before they speak, even to the point of allowing five seconds or more to elapse before answering a question. It appears that, in a courtroom and perhaps elsewhere, the thoughtful, deliberate respondent is likely to be misunderstood as being dishonest.

Of course, it is possible to delay one's response indefinitely, that is, to respond to a question or comment with silence. The silent response can have many different meanings depending on the social and cultural context. In some societies, silent responses to yes–no questions generally mean "yes" and in others silence is normally taken to mean "no." Although I know of no systematic study of the silent response in American society, it appears from casual observation that a silent response is most often taken as a "no." Saville-Troike (1985:8) provides the following example of silence as an implicit negative response. Although this example appears to have been taken from another culture, it exemplifies an interaction that could very well have taken place in the United States.

> A: We've received word that four Tanzanian acquaintances from out of town will be arriving tomorrow. But, with our large family, we have no room to accommodate them. (Implied request: 'Would you help us out.')
> B: [Silence; not accompanied by any distinctive gesture or facial expression] (Denial: 'I don't want to' or 'I don't have any room either')
> A: What do you think?
> B: Yes, that is a problem. Were you able to finish that report we were working on this morning?

Since a silent response can mean that the other did not hear or was not attending to what was said, it is common to follow such a silent response by either repeating what was said or elaborating on it. This is a way of not only assuring that the other heard and understood what was said, but also of implying to the other that a silent response is unsatisfactory. Notice in this example that B's response of acknowledging the problem and then changing the subject served to reinforce the negative intention of the silent response. Not only cultures, but also individuals, differ in their use of and interpretation of silent responses. Individuals who tend to be very direct and explicit might not be as sensitive as others to the implicit meaning of silent responses. Those who are more direct in making requests are also probably less likely to understand that a statement such as A's opening announcement constitutes a request that requires a verbal response. If not, their silence might not mean "no," but simply, "I have no advice to offer you in this situation."

Norms of silence extend beyond the particular interaction and social setting to the social identities of the interactants. It is still a common belief among some Americans that children should be seen and not heard. Although that belief is not widely held in the youth and child-centered culture of late twentieth-century America, it is still the norm in various other cultures around the world. Despite the relative aversion Americans have for ritual, it is still a commonly acknowledged if not practiced ritual for brides and grooms not to talk to each other on their wedding day. Other categories of people who routinely maintain long periods of silence in the presence of others are psychotherapists, custodial workers, bus drivers, and strangers.

The interesting thing about silence is that, because it explicitly expresses nothing, its implicit meaning must be derived solely from the social context in which it occurs. That is why silence can imply subordination, as when the worker silently receives instructions from the boss, or as dominance, as when the expert withholds approval by remaining silent while others attempt to make their point. Because of the highly contextual nature of the meaning of silence, it is necessary that the interpretation of silence be informed by a high degree of familiarity with the situation in which it occurs. This is nowhere clearer than in the relationship between gender and silence. The cultural stereotypes of the strong silent man and the overly chatty women are still very much alive. Perhaps because of this cultural belief that females are too talkative, numerous studies provide evidence that girls are more likely to be socialized to remain silent while boys are taught to express their ideas openly. It appears that, despite these cultural stereotypes, socialization does produce more talkative males and more silent females. Jennifer Coates (1986) cites studies that show consistently and in a variety of social settings that men talk more than women.

Although, in general, men talk more than women, there is also evidence that men and women differ markedly in the way they use silence in conversations. Zimmerman and West (1975) found that in mixed-sex conversations men were more likely to interrupt women, while women were more likely to sit silently until men were finished speaking. They also found that men allowed a longer silence before uttering minimal responses (such as, "yeah" or "mm-hm"). Minimal responses imply interest and attention on the part of the listener. Delaying such responses might give the impression that the listener does not understand or is not interested in what is being said, which can create social anxiety on the part of the speaker.

It is clear that gender differences in the use of silence could and sometimes do produce significant misunderstandings between men and women. What is interesting, however, is that these patterns have become such an accepted part of male–female interactions that they often go unnoticed. Whether noticed or not, however, they can seriously influence attributions of competence and concern. In the final chapter, I will attempt to explain in more detail some of the causes and effects of gender differences in the use of talk and silence.

Conclusion: Why the "Truth" Is So Hard to Come By

As humans we are naturally curious about the causes of events. In trying to understand events that are brought about by human action, our curiosity often turns to the question of motives. Why people do the things they do is not only a preoccupation of students of the behavioral and social sciences, it is also a topic of high priority in everyday discourse. In this chapter we have seen that our interpretation of the meaning and causes of social events is biased in a number of ways. Because of the complexity of interpreting human actions, we often employ shortcuts, what social psychologists call "judgment heuristics." These heuristics allow us to make quick judgments about the causes of routine everyday events, without having to engage in serious contemplation. The use of such shortcuts, however, introduces various biases into the process that interfere with our ability to accurately understand the meaning of and motives behind various acts.

Moreover, even when we consciously contemplate the meanings and motives associated with social acts, the attribution process is likely to be biased in a variety of ways. Such biases in our ability to accurately utilize social cues to interpret the meaning and causes of behavior frequently lead to systematic attribution errors. These errors are often the result of our predisposition to (1) ignore the influence of situational or environmental influences on the actions of others, (2) blame our own failures on situational constraints and attribute our successes to such internal factors as ability and hard work, and (3) seek explanations that cast a favorable light on those we perceive to be like ourselves and an unfavorable light on those we perceive to be different from ourselves. Such biases carry the benefit of protecting our self-esteem and our personal relationships with significant others. Unfortunately for them, some individuals err in the opposite direction and fall victim to biases that work to their own detriment. For example, the depressive attributional style is associated with such costs as depression and low self-esteem. Thus, whether we employ attributional biases that flatter or demean, the result is that we are often led to false understandings about ourselves and others.

The interpretation of words and actions, however, is no more difficult and subject to bias than is the interpretation of silence and inaction. As part of our culture, Americans tend to value sound over silence and are often suspicious of those who are quiet and uncommunicative. Of course, the extent to which silence is considered appropriate for a given person in a given situation will vary by gender, social class, and cultural grouping, and ignorance of such group differences can lead to serious misunderstandings of why individuals act or don't act and why they speak or remain silent.

By now, the ways in which and the reasons why we misinterpret the actions of others should be fairly clear. Moreover, understanding the systematic biases in the way we interpret actions or inactions suggests something about the types of misinterpretation that can result. For example, one basic type suggested by the discussion in this chapter is what we might call the "actor–situation misinterpretation." That is, we often misinterpret the meaning or motive of an action by overemphasizing individual intentionality and failing to take adequate account of the situational factors that influence behavior. However, the study of attributional biases suggests very little about one of the most fundamental types of interpretational problems, the tendency to overinterpret or underinterpret the meaning and significance of another person's actions. In the next chapter I will conclude the discussion of interpretation by taking up that issue in some detail.

The Self-Monitoring Scale

The statements on the following pages concern your personal reactions to a number of different situations. No two statements are exactly alike, so consider each statement carefully before answering. If a statement is true or mostly true as applied to you, place a T beside the statement. If a statement is false or mostly false as applied to you, place an F beside the statement. It is important that you answer as frankly and as honestly as you can.

1. I find it hard to imitate the behavior of other people.
2. My behavior is usually an expression of my true inner feelings, attitudes, and beliefs.
3. At parties and social gatherings, I do not attempt to do or say things that others will like.
4. I can only argue for ideas I already believe.
5. I can make impromptu speeches even on topics about which I have almost no information.
6. I guess I put on a show to impress or entertain people.
7. When I am uncertain how to act in a social situation, I look to the behavior of the others for cues.
8. I would probably make a good actor.
9. I rarely seek the advice of my friends to choose movies, books, or music.
10. I sometimes appear to others to be experiencing deeper emotions than I actually am.
11. I laugh more when I watch a comedy with others than when alone.
12. In a group of people I am rarely the center of attention.
13. In different situations and with different people, I often pretend to be having a good time.
14. I am not particularly good at making other people like me.
15. Even if I am not enjoying myself, I often pretend to be having a good time.

16. *I'm not always the person I appear to be.*
17. *I would not change my opinions (or the way I do things) in order to please other people or win their favor.*
18. *I have considered being an entertainer.*
19. *In order to get along and be liked, I tend to be what people expect me to be rather than anything else.*
20. *I have never been good at games like charades or improvisational acting.*
21. *I have trouble changing my behavior to suit different people and different situations.*
22. *At a party I let others keep the jokes and stories going.*
23. *I feel a bit awkward and do not show up quite as well as I should.*
24. *I can look anyone in the eye and tell a lie with a straight face (if for a right end).*
25. *I may deceive people by being friendly when I really dislike them.*

Answer key for Self-Monitoring Scale (these are the answers that indicate high self-monitoring):

1. *F*	6. *T*	11. *T*	16. *T*	21. *F*
2. *F*	7. *T*	12. *F*	17. *F*	22. *F*
3. *F*	8. *T*	13. *T*	18. *T*	23. *F*
4. *F*	9. *F*	14. *F*	19. *T*	24. *T*
5. *T*	10. *T*	15. *T*	20. *F*	25. *T*

Add up the number of your answers that agree with the answer key. The higher the number of matching answers, the higher your self-monitoring score.

5

Modest Actions,

Monumental

Misunderstandings [1]

*Great literature is simply language
charged with meaning to the utmost
possible degree.*

EZRA POUND, *American poet*

That which makes great literature often makes unfortunate discourse.
During a speech to the American Enterprise Institute on December 5, 1996, Federal Reserve Chair Alan Greenspan posed the following questions: "How do we know when irrational exuberance has unduly escalated asset values, which then become the subject of unexpected and prolonged contractions, as they have in Japan over the past decade? And how do we factor that assessment into monetary policy?"

In the fascinating psychological world of the stock market, the mere suggestion by someone of Greenspan's economic power that the market might be due for a fall can produce a familiar self-fulfilling prophecy, whereby stockholders attempting to sell before their current holdings became devalued produce that very devaluation. As a result, those somewhat slower on the draw suffer the consequences. No doubt stockbrokers, who stand to gain whether stocks are bought or sold, do little to quell such fears. Whether Greenspan anticipated the far-reaching effect of his comments is unknown, but it is unlikely that even he imagined just what a dramatic and immediate impact his words would have. It is often the unfortunate plight of those in positions of authority that casual comments are accorded significance well beyond their intentions, although it is also true that such individuals can occasionally exploit this fact to their advantage.

The problem of assessing the significance of action also produces the opposite effect; words and deeds that are intended to carry great significance are sometimes ignored or casually dismissed. Although this can happen to anyone, it is more often the dilemma of those of lesser status. All actions—verbal and nonverbal, serious and facetious—can be intended to carry messages of great significance or of very little import, and can likewise be interpreted at multiple levels. The result is that many misunderstandings occur because observers over- or underinterpret the actions of others (Young 1995a). In order to clarify what I mean by levels of action, it will first be necessary to explain, in a general sense, the kinds of things actions accomplish.

Meanings and Effects: What Actions Do

John is walking down the street when he recognizes Kathy from a distance and waves. Kathy hesitates, then tentatively returns the gesture as they continue on their respective paths. How do we make sense of this hesitant and less-than-enthusiastic response to such a common action? A number of plausible explanations could be offered, but the answer is likely to lie in the meaning Kathy attributed to the wave. Did John actually wave his arm, or was he simply raising his hand to block the sun? If he was waving, was he waving to Kathy or someone else? If he was waving to Kathy, did she recognize him, and if she did, did she fear that returning the gesture would lead to a lengthy conversation she had no time for? Suppose the two had had an unpleasant exchange the day before. Was the wave intended sarcastically, repentantly, or casually?

This particular interaction illustrates the fact that all actions can be interpreted at different levels of meaning. At the most basic level, actions can be interpreted and described in purely *physical* terms. The action of hailing a cab, for example, could be described thus: "I stepped forward, placing my right foot on the street, leaving the left on the sidewalk, looked directly at the oncoming cab, raised both hands above my head, lowered them approximately forty-five degrees, and repeated this motion rapidly three times." Actions that are interpreted in purely physical terms are likely to elicit quite different responses from those interpreted at a more social level. Cab drivers who observe this kind of gesturing but do not interpret such actions as they are intended will leave would-be passengers frustrated and stranded. Likewise, if I see a student raise her hand in class but interpret it as a purely physical action, such as stretching, I will not acknowledge the student as someone who has something to say. Actions interpreted as purely physical acts are not perceived as attempts to communicate social messages; thus we are inclined to pay them little attention.

In contrast, what I will call "*generalized* actions" are those that are seen as attempts to communicate something specific. The problem with generalized actions, however, is that the observer is unsure of precisely what they are supposed to mean. Suppose that during an office meeting Frank notices Jim look at Beth and nod. Does this nod of the head signal that Jim agrees with the point the speaker just made, or does it signal the initiation of some strategic plan he and Beth have worked out in advance? Frank might be fairly certain that it signals something of social significance (that is, Jim is not simply falling asleep), but without more information and interpretation, he cannot be sure what it means. Likewise, simple utterances such as "yes" can signal agreement or simply indicate that the listener is paying attention. Because generalized actions are assumed to communicate something the observer cannot interpret, they tend to grab and hold our attention as we struggle to make sense of them.

The third level of action is the *implicative* level. Unlike ambiguous generalized actions, implicative actions are those to which we are able to attribute precise meaning. Often, more important than the meaning itself is the fact that implicative actions are assumed to indicate specific motives or states of mind on the part of actors. To say that John flirted with Kathy, for example, is to suggest that John's actions were motivated by a desire to let Kathy know that he found her attractive. For actions to be interpreted at the implicative level, observers must do a fair amount of interpretation. Noticing that John blinked one of his eyes while looking at Kathy (a physical action) requires no interpretation. Concluding that this action constituted a wink (generalized action) requires some interpretive work. Concluding, on the basis of a wink, that John was flirting with Kathy involves even more interpretation. After all, a wink can also indicate, among other things, that the two share knowledge of which others are not aware. Whether observers interpret a wink as meaning one thing or another depends on other information available to them.

Analyzing all the information necessary to interpret an action at the implicative level is a complex cognitive process. However, because our culture supplies us with a large set of standardized scripts with which we can quickly compare individual actions, categorizing an action as having one implication or another is greatly simplified. The down side of such categorical interpretations, however, is that misunderstandings are likely to develop if actions deviate much from standard scripts. For example, if John were twenty-five years old and Kathy were sixty, most observers would interpret John's wink as something other than a romantic gesture, since our cultural scripts for flirtatious winks do not readily accommodate the possibility of romantic relationships between twenty-five-year-old men and sixty-year-old women.

Once actions have been interpreted, they may have dramatic effects on observers or they may have little or no effect at all. Ordinary actions, such as saying hello to those we encounter, paying for things we have purchased at the grocery store, or performing routine tasks at work do little to alter the future of those to whom they are directed. Other times, however, actions can have profound effects on others. Saying hello to someone we have refused to speak to for years, paying for a major purchase to an individual who stands to make a considerable personal profit on the sale, or performing work tasks that can mean the difference between being promoted and being fired are all actions that are likely to have significant consequences for ourselves and/or others involved. Thus, I use the term *consequential* actions to represent the highest or most complex level of action. Consequential actions share all the characteristics of implicative actions. However, they are not defined solely by their meaning, but also by the effects they have on observers. Greetings are consequential if and only if they are interpreted as more than just routine, thereby making those who are greeted happy, honored, suspicious, or in some other way mentally or emotionally different from how they were before the greeting.

Actions of this sort can produce two types of consequences. *Personal consequences* are those that somehow affect the life of the observer but do not alter the relationship between the actor and the observer. If people we love pay us compliments, they are likely to make us feel good, but they are unlikely to alter our relationships with them. After all, we expect occasional compliments from those we love. Compliments from those we perceive as especially objective or critical, however, can make our day. In addition to such personal effects, actions often have *interpersonal consequences;* that is, they affect the relationship between the actor and the observer. Receiving a compliment from someone we don't particularly like, for example, might increase our liking for them and thus influence our future relationship.

To summarize, all actions can be described and may be interpreted at a physical, generalized, implicative, or consequential level. As we move from the physical to the generalized, to the implicative, more information is necessary and additional interpretation is involved. Finally, consequential actions are distinguished from others by virtue of the significance of the effects they have on observers or the relationship between actors and observers.

Intentions, Interpretations, and the Creation of Misunderstandings

It is clear that actions intended at one level are sometimes interpreted at another level. Likewise, many misunderstandings are the result of the fact that actions intended at one level are interpreted at another. All the possible types of misunderstanding that can result from over- or underinterpretation are displayed in Table 1. As the table shows, observers might recognize any action on the part of actors in physical, generalized, implicative, or consequential terms. However, actors do not normally intend for their actions to be interpreted at a generalized level. Most physical actions are performed with little or no regard for the way others might interpret them. All social actions, however, are performed with the expectation that others will interpret them in a particular way. For example, I might move my head in a nodding fashion to relieve neck tension or place my hand in a waving position in order to block the sun, but I do not nod or wave at another person unless I intend it to have a particular meaning to someone. Thus, although actions may be interpreted at any of the four levels discussed above, actions are never intended at a generalized level. As a result, there is a certain asymmetry between the levels at which actions may be intended by actors and the levels at which they might be recognized by observers.

This asymmetry between levels of intention and levels of interpretation is reflected in Table 1. The cells of the table designated by two capital letters represent the types of misunderstandings that can result from the mismatch between actors' intentions and observers' interpretations. Before discussing these different types of misunderstanding, I should make a few other points. First, as discussed above, no actions are intended as generalized actions. Second, any actions interpreted as generalized actions result in nonunderstandings. This is because both understandings and misunderstandings—in contrast to nonunderstandings—imply that the action has

UNDERSTANDING

Table 1. Intended Versus Recognized Level of Action

Level of Action as Interpreted by Observer	Level of Action Assumed or Intended by Actor		
	Physical (P)	Implicative (I)	Consequential (C)
Physical	Possible Understanding	I P	C P
Generalized	Non-understanding	Non-understanding	Non-understanding
Implicative	P I	Possible Understanding	C I
Consequential	P C	I C	Possible Understanding

a particular meaning for observers. Because generalized actions are completely ambiguous to observers, they cannot be misunderstood; they can only be not understood. Finally, although understanding can exist only when actions are interpreted at the same level at which they were intended, interpreting an act at the appropriate level does not guarantee that the act has been correctly understood. For example, if John's flirtatious wink is correctly perceived as an implicative action, the observer might still be wrong about exactly what it implies. Thus, I have used the term *possible understanding* to describe situations in which intention and interpretation levels match.

The cells in the table representing misunderstandings are identified with the first letters of the level of intention and the level of interpretation, respectively. The two misunderstanding cells in the upper right corner of the table (IP and CP) and the CI cell represent situations in which the actions of the actor have been underinterpreted, whereas the three cells in the lower left (PI, PC, and IC) are all the result of overinterpretations on the part of observers. For example, an IP misunderstanding would be one in which an actor intends the action to have specific social meaning, but the observer misinterprets the action as being purely physical. If a listener clears her throat to signal to the speaker to beware of what he says, but the speaker interprets the gesture as nothing more than an effort to cope with a congested throat, he has misunderstood the gesture by underinterpreting it. On the other hand, a PI misunderstanding would result if a speaker interpreted a purely physical clearing of the throat as a signal by the observer that the speaker should watch what he says. Likewise, an IC misunderstanding suggests that the observer has overinterpreted an action that was intended to imply something of relatively minor personal or interpersonal consequence to mean something more consequential. The following is an example of a PC misunderstanding.

> The other night in class I hiccuped during a presentation being given by another girl in the class. You have to understand that my hiccups can sound very strange, sort of like a gasp. That would have been embarrassing enough, but it just so happened that I hiccuped right when she was giving her opinion on something kind of controversial, so she was probably feeling a little self-conscious about it anyhow. Well, it was clear from her reaction and the reaction of others that they thought my hiccup was a gasp expressing my disapproval or disagreement with what she said. That made me feel really embarrassed, so I was quick to apologize and assure her that it was just a hiccup.

As this story suggests, producing inadvertent bodily noises in public can be embarrassing enough on its own. What is also clear, however, is that the major source of embarrassment here was the fact that the physical act of hiccuping was interpreted as the social act of vocally disapproving, an act that would have had negative consequences for both the self-esteem of the speaker and the future relationship of the two individuals.

Because physical actions are usually easy to distinguish from social ones, they are less likely to be interpreted at another level. Distinguishing between levels of social action, however, is somewhat more difficult. Consider the following example of an IC misunderstanding, supplied by another student.

> About two years ago, New Year's Eve, a male friend and I had a terrible misunderstanding concerning our relationship that night. First of all, I asked him if he wanted to go out. He said he had never been out on NYE before. I had not made any plans, so I thought it would be fun to go celebrate together. The night was a disaster. He assumed that we were on a date. We were not. I was only concerned about being a good friend. I did not want a serious relationship with him. Everything I did he took as a sign that I liked him. I was just being nice. I was treating him as I treated everyone else. I even told him point blank that I didn't like him in that way. To this day, I don't know how to act around him. If I'm nice, I feel he thinks I like him [romantically], and if I'm mean, I feel like he thinks I'm weird. Needless to say, we are not the friends we used to be.

In this example, the act of asking an opposite-sex friend to go out on New Year's Eve was not expected to have significant interpersonal consequences. The narrator was simply suggesting that since neither had plans, maybe they should celebrate the new year together. Unfortunately, her friend interpreted the invitation as an act that had significant consequences for their relationship. Ironically, because of the misunderstanding, the evening did have lasting consequences for their relationship, but not of the kind initially imagined by the friend.

Am I Paranoid or Just Powerless?
Overinterpreting and Underinterpreting Actions

There are many specific reasons why a particular action might be over- or underinterpreted. In a general sense, however, there are two types of causes: personal and interpersonal. By personal causes, I mean that some individuals are more inclined than others to have difficulty finding the appropriate level of interpretation. People who suffer from paranoia, for example, have a persistent tendency to overinterpret the actions of others. Believing that the actions of others have serious personal consequences for oneself is a major part of paranoia. This is not to say that anyone who has a tendency to overinterpret the actions of others is paranoid. Often there are understandable interpersonal reasons for such interpretations. As Charles Berger (1979) suggests, individuals who are highly dependent on others are likely to attach great significance to the actions of those upon whom they are dependent, and justifiably so. Young children, for example, often act as though dire consequences would ensue if their parents left them alone, even momentarily. Although adults often laugh at such reactions, from the point of view of the dependent child, who does not know when the parents will return or what might happen while they are gone, such concerns are not unreasonable. Dependent or insecure adults may react similarly to the idea of their partner leaving them to spend time with others, regardless of how legitimate the reason. Dependence is often linked to powerlessness, and the actions of powerful individuals really do tend to have more significant consequences than those of the less powerful individuals. For example, although most of the actions of patients have relatively minor consequences for the physicians upon whom they depend, the actions of the doctors can have life-or-death consequences for their patients.

As a result of the greater consequentiality of the acts of the more powerful interactant, situations that involve interactions between subordinates and those with power over them tend to motivate the less powerful individuals to closely monitor their own actions and those of the other. Such monitoring is motivated by the desire to avoid being misunderstood and the parallel need to understand the full implications of the other's actions. Situations that tend to produce these kinds of misunderstandings are found in the lower left corner of Table 1. In contrast, situations that are less personally consequential for the observer will be more likely to produce underinterpretations and lead to the type of misunderstandings found in the other cells of the table.

The Problem with Fixing It

Actors and observers don't always devote the same measure of attention to an interaction. As a result, as actors we do not always consciously think about our intentions before we act. Before we sigh, yawn, or stretch, for example, we are not likely to think about how such physical acts will be interpreted by others. However, upon realizing that our actions have been misinterpreted, we become acutely aware of what impressions we did not intend to give. Thus, whether or not we consciously intended an action to carry a particular level of meaning, we are quick to declare that certain meanings were not our intention.

In general, the diligence with which we monitor actions, both our own and those of others, is related to the importance of the interaction for us. As I suggested in the previous section, in situations that we expect to be highly consequential, we tend to be especially attentive to the more subtle aspects of the other's behavior and are thus more sensitive to the implications of all his or her actions. On such occasions we also tend to be more careful in orchestrating our own acts, choosing our words carefully, and plotting our moves more methodically than usual. Because of this enhanced attention to detail and subtlety, we are more likely than our less invested interaction partner to recognize misunderstandings when they do occur.

Whether a misunderstanding is first recognized by an actor or an observer has important implications for the future of the interaction. Observers who realize they have misunderstood the actions of another can simply adjust their thinking to bring it into line with newly discovered information. When actors are the first to recognize that they have been misunderstood, however, they must take concrete action in order to rectify the situation, and sometimes this can be a traumatic realization. As the work of psychologist Arnold Buss (1980) suggests, the realization that we must actively work to correct a misunderstanding is likely to produce a degree of anxiety. In order to take corrective actions, we often must disrupt the flow of interaction and take it in a new and probably uncomfortable direction. This alone can make us somewhat uneasy, but such uneasiness will be exaggerated by any uncertainty we might have over whether or not the action we are contemplating will be considered appropriate. This is one of the reasons why realizing that we have been misunderstood is normally more bothersome than realizing that we have misunderstood someone else. In the face of such a dilemma, whether or not we take any action at all depends largely on whether the anxiety of allowing the other's misunderstanding of our actions to persist is greater or less than the anxiety created by imagining the other's reaction to our efforts to clarify the situation.

Conclusion: Truth and Consequences

Actions can be intended as physical, implicative, or consequential and can be interpreted as either physical, generalized, implicative, or consequential. When words or deeds are intended at one level but are interpreted at another—that is, when we read too much or too little into each other's actions, misunderstanding results. Casual or innocent comments that are overinterpreted can result in such interpersonal problems as embarrassment, resentment, or outright conflict. Although discovering that their actions have been underinterpreted is likely to be somewhat less problematic at the interpersonal level, this kind of misunderstanding nevertheless can be extremely frustrating for actors who might be left wondering just how obvious they have to be to get their point across.

Whether we recognize such discrepancies between our intentions and others' interpretations depends largely on how closely we monitor the situation, and that often depends on how much we have to gain or lose from the interaction. In general, interactions among those with different amounts of social power are more consequential for less powerful individuals. As a result, they will typically monitor their own actions and those of the other more carefully, and, thus, will be more likely than the other to recognize when they have been misunderstood. Although such a realization is beneficial in that it allows them the opportunity to clarify things, it may, for that very reason, create extreme anxiety. After all, actions aimed at clarification could also be misunderstood, thus making bad matters worse. Moreover, if actors are wrong in their perception that they have been misunderstood, clarification efforts will be inappropriate, which in turn might make the other feel insulted or make the actor appear foolish. Thus, while problematic for anyone, the perception of having been misunderstood can be especially traumatic for those of a subordinate status.

A common way of alleviating some of the anxiety associated with face-to-face interaction is to provide feedback to the other. Feedback allows actors to assess whether or not they are being understood. We have all had the unpleasant and somewhat intimidating experience of interacting with the type of person who provides little or no feedback as we struggle to express ourselves. When conversing with anyone, but especially those of lower status, we should be aware of the need to occasionally reassure them that we understand what they are communicating. However, it is wise to be aware of how we express our understanding. A common way of doing so is by nodding and using such verbal affirmative responses as "yes" or "O.K." Unfortunately, such responses can be interpreted as signs of agreement rather than interest or understanding. More explicit responses, such as "I understand" or "I see what you mean," are less likely to be misunderstood. As we will see in the final chapter, this seemingly minor distinction can be especially important in interactions between men and women. Likewise, we should be willing to politely ask for clarifications when necessary. Avoiding misunderstandings is often easier and almost always less stressful than attempting to correct them. This assumes, of course, that we want to reduce the stress of those with whom we interact.

Notes

1. For a more elaborate and scholarly treatment of this topic, see Young (1995a).

6

The

Consummation

and the

Aftermath

Behavioral

Responses

and Emotional Reactions

*Men's actions are too strong for them.
Show me a man who has acted, and who
has not been the victim and slave of his
action.*

RALPH WALDO EMERSON, *American poet*

Imagine the following scenario. A store customer approaches a cashier and hands her an item she wishes to buy. The cashier enters the purchase into the computer, looks up, and says to the customer: "That will be seven sixty-five please." As the cashier bags the merchandise, the customer counts out six dollars and seventy-five cents and places it on the counter. After counting the money, the cashier looks back at the customer, smiles, and says, "That was seven sixty-five." "Oh, I'm sorry," explains the blushing customer as she hurriedly hands over another two dollars, "I thought you said six seventy-five." The cashier takes the money, smiles, enters the appropriate numbers into the keyboard, retrieves a dollar and a dime from the register drawer, and hands the change to the customer. The customer takes the money and the receipt, realizes that she only needed to give the cashier one additional dollar, and blushes again. Looking down, she stuffs the money and receipt into her purse and makes a hasty retreat.

Although this misunderstanding causes no major problems and is not likely to be remembered by either party for very long, it nevertheless demonstrates the dynamic nature of the misunderstanding process. In addition to containing the essential elements of action, perception, and interpretation, which were discussed in earlier chapters, it also reveals both the form and function of the *response,* which is the final necessary step in the misunderstanding process.

The action that initiates this particular misunderstanding sequence is the cashier's statement: "That will be seven sixty-five, please." The customer misperceives the cashier's words as "that will be six seventy-five, please," and interprets what she has heard to mean "you owe six dollars and seventy-five cents." As the cashier begins to bag the merchandise, she does not realize that the customer has misunderstood what she said. She discovers that only when the customer responds to her comment by giving her less than the amount of the purchase. Interactants become aware of misunderstandings only through the responses that have been generated by misperceptions and misinterpretations. Notice that it was only because the customer's response was not properly coordinated with the cashier's initial action that the cashier was alerted to the misunderstanding. If the customer had used a ten-dollar bill or credit card to pay, the misunderstanding never would have come to light. No doubt, many misunderstandings occur in daily life without anyone ever knowing. Most misunderstandings become known and shared experiences only through *miscoordinated responses.* Such responses, which are out of synch with the original action, serve as vital hints to actors that their actions have been misunderstood.

Misperceptions and misinterpretations often lead to miscoordinated actions that create awkward moments or occasionally outright conflict. Ironically, however, awkwardness and conflict are sometimes avoided precisely because of misunderstandings. For example, a slightly veiled insult that is not perceived as an insult will have little or no influence on the flow of interaction. Actor Jim Nabors is famous for his television portrayal of Gomer Pyle, a good-hearted but simple-minded U.S. Marine private who blissfully endured the insults of Sergeant Carter because he failed to understand that they were intended as insults. In fact, it was a persistent source of consternation for Carter that his barbs were incapable of intimidating the oblivious Pyle or disrupting his course of action.

Insults, slights, snubs, or other expressions of negative feelings will not disrupt interaction unless and until they are understood as disparaging. However, other kinds of misunderstandings—especially those involving factual information—can have immediate negative consequences. I recently had a driving experience that illustrates this point. Before turning onto a busy street from a place where I could not see in both directions, I asked the person sitting in the passenger seat, "How does it look over there? Can I go?" Unfortunately, although she said, "No!" I heard it as "Go!" My response was nearly catastrophic as we were barely able to avoid a collision with an oncoming car.

Open Mouth, Insert Foot: Hazards of Miscoordinated Responses

Social interaction is one-half action and one-half reaction. Humans are constantly altering their behavior in order to coordinate it with the actions of others. Misunderstandings create interactional chaos by inducing responses that are not coordinated with the actions they follow. The first clear indication that a misunderstanding has occurred is found in the response of the person who has misunderstood. When actions appear inappropriate, our responses tend to be cautious as we attempt to collect additional information and figure out what is going on. When actions appear situationally appropriate, however, we tend to respond quickly, decisively, and without further interpretation. Thus, whether we are driving a car or carrying on a casual conversation, the more appropriate the actions of others appear, if we have misunderstood them, the more likely we are to respond in a way that seems appropriate to us but inappropriate to the other. Consider the following example.

At six feet four inches tall, Brian literally stands well above the conversation in many situations. He has an especially difficult time conversing with people in situations where there is lots of background noise. Rather than constantly asking people to repeat themselves or talk louder, he has learned to read the body language of speakers and other listeners in order to respond in ways that seem appropriate. Although this strategy usually works, it occasionally fails miserably, and he hears just well enough to get himself into trouble. This happened recently at a party he was attending. He was having a conversation with a couple who were telling a story about their teenage daughter, who had disappeared for several hours earlier that day. Just as they were about to start calling around for her, their seven-year-old son informed them that "she had gone to a mall with some friends." As he listened to the story, Brian heard the word *mall* as *ball*, and laughingly responded with, "Yeah! Right! In the middle of the afternoon!" "Well," said the mother, looking somewhat surprised, "they often do that on Saturday afternoon." As Brian was trying to figure out whether ballroom dancing had become the latest craze among teenagers or whether this was just a strange family he was dealing with, something else was said that made him realize he must have misunderstood something. Once he realized that, he was able to quickly figure out what he should have heard.

What made this misunderstanding possible was that the comment "she had gone to a ball with some friends" made just enough sense to be misleading. If he had perceived the mother to have said "she had gone to a *small* with some friends," a statement that makes no sense, Brian would have probably asked for clarification before responding. Instead, he incorrectly interpreted what he heard as an awkward lie told by a protective seven-year-old brother. Whenever misperceptions and misinterpretations make no sense to observers, their experience is one of nonunderstanding, and when things make no sense, interaction becomes virtually frozen while observers attempt to make sense of things. As we saw in Chapter 1, misunderstood actions always make sense, and precisely because of that, they often produce responses that don't. Nevertheless, numerous studies of conversation reveal the amazing ability of humans to make sense of nonsense. This ability allows many conversations to continue for several turns before the interactants realize that they have been talking past each other. In fact, after relatively brief conversations, actors might never realize that they have completely misunderstood one another.

A study by Harold Garfinkel (1967) vividly illustrates the ability of people to make sense of nonsense. In an experiment conducted at UCLA, student subjects were told that research was being done on a new psychotherapy technique which involved subjects' asking a counselor a series of questions that could be answered with a simple "yes" or "no." Unbeknownst to subjects, the counselors' answers were predetermined and thus completely random. Nevertheless, subjects were able to interpret the answers in such a way as to render them germane to their particular problems. After the counseling session subjects expressed the belief that the counselors had understood and helped them work through their problems.

Responding to the Outrageous:
Strategies for Avoiding Miscoordinated Responses

Misunderstood comments or actions that are recognized as improper or out of place create a different kind of problem for observers, who must attempt to formulate appropriate responses to inappropriate acts. In some cases, however, actions *appear* inappropriate only because they have been misunderstood. Reactions based on misunderstandings, therefore, are likely to appear inappropriate to the original actor. As a result, interactants who are both acting and responding in ways that seem appropriate to them will appear inappropriate to each other. What a mess!

Inappropriate acts pose serious threats to social interaction. Thus, it is not surprising that humans have developed a variety of strategies for dealing with them. One of the most common strategies is to simply ignore perceived improprieties in the hope that they will not be repeated. Pretending that untoward acts never occurred is more common in some cultural and situational contexts than in others. For example, this practice is more common among adult peers than among childhood or adolescent peer groups. Young children are especially quick to criticize peers whose behavior they consider out of line. Comments such as "No, that's wrong" or "That's not how you do it" are common among children, who have not yet learned the subtleties of politeness. According to social psychologist John Kinch (1973), however, receiving such criticism from other children teaches the child the importance of seeing things from the perspective of the other and helps him or her learn valuable role-taking skills. Although it will never be easy to accept criticism, being criticized is a common, accepted, and valuable part of the childhood experience. As we mature into young adults and learn to behave consistently in ways others consider more or less appropriate, we are subjected to less and less overt criticism from older adults and from peers. As criticism from others becomes less common, however, we become more emotionally sensitive to it, if and when it does occur. Such increased sensitivity to criticism from others makes most of us more tolerant of others who make mistakes and less inclined to overtly criticize them, knowing all too well that the shoe often changes feet. Moreover, unlike young children, adults know that others do not necessarily share their perceptions of reality. This in turn leads to the realization that those who decline opportunities to challenge the untoward behavior of others not only reduce their own chances of being criticized, they also protect themselves from having their perceptions of reality challenged by anyone who might have a different view of things. There is a certain irony in all this, for by challenging perceived improprieties, children allow each other the chance to see that their actions have been misunderstood. By ignoring such behavior, however, adults who have been misunderstood are not afforded that opportunity by their more civilized peers.

An alternative to ignoring perceived improprieties, especially in talk, is to employ *hedging* actions. Hedging actions are intentionally ambiguous responses that are used when observers find it difficult to ignore untoward acts but do not want to directly confront actors. Actors sometimes make it impossible to ignore them, as when they explicitly ask for confirmation with such phrases as "Isn't that right?" or "Don't you agree?" Rather than answering directly, we might abruptly change the subject or use such non-committal replies as, "Well, I don't know," or simply "ummm." The problem with hedging responses is that because they do not explicitly confront or confirm the perceived untoward behavior, different actors will interpret them differently. The assertive actor is likely to take anything less than an outright rebuke as a confirmation, whereas the timid actor is likely to take anything less than an obvious confirmation as a rebuke. I have talked to numerous people who have been in otherwise pleasant situations in which someone made an uninvited and unappreciated racial or ethnic slur. These comments, usually directed at groups not represented in the immediate situation, are often made in such a way as to invite a response. This places observers in the uncomfortable position of having to confront someone who may have been quite congenial to everyone present, even though they have expressed attitudes that are not considered acceptable to those same listeners. It appears that in situations such as this, many people try to ignore the insulting comment or respond in a very noncommittal way, hoping that the speaker gets the hint. Because of their inherent ambiguity, however, hedged responses can easily lead to further misunderstandings, as when prejudiced individuals assume that anyone who does not openly disagree with them must surely agree.

There is less danger of the proliferation of misunderstandings when observers respond directly to the perceived impropriety. Responses such as "What did you say?" "What do you mean?" "Do you really believe that?" "Why do you say that?" "Why did you do that?" "I disagree!" or simply "No!" directly challenge the action, although some do it more aggressively than others. Direct challenges usually invite some form of explanation, justification, excuse, or apology from the actor. As mentioned above, the advantage of challenges is that they allow the actor to clear up any possible misunderstanding. The disadvantage, of course, is that they can lead to open conflict.

As much as we might want to avoid directly confronting people when they act inappropriately, it is sometimes necessary. Here is one of the many areas of social interaction where style is often more important than content. If we are too direct, we run the risk of offending the actor and creating conflict, but if we are too indirect, the actor may not take our hint and continue or repeat the offensive behavior. Knowledge of the other person is vital in choosing the right strategy, because some people are much more sensitive to criticism than others. No matter who we are dealing with, however, it is always important to make it clear that we are critiquing the action rather than the person. Qualifying phrases, such as "I know you would never do anything to intentionally hurt my feelings," go a long way toward softening the blow of the challenges that follow them. Also remember the importance of timing, which was discussed in Chapter 2.

Validating Misunderstandings: The Self-Fulfilling Prophecy

Whenever we misunderstand an action, our responses are essentially responses to something different from what was intended. When we hear a statement incorrectly, we hear something that was not said, something that exists only in our mind. As a result, responses that are rooted in misunderstandings are inherently misguided. No matter how unrealistic the understandings on which responses are based, however, the responses themselves are real and instantly become an important part of the ongoing social situation. One of the unfortunate results of misunderstandings is that they can set in motion a series of responses and actions that reinforce the misunderstanding. For example, if I misunderstand an innocent comment as an insult and respond with what I consider a counterinsult, that is likely to lead the original actor, who sees no justification for my insult, to retaliate. That retaliation, unfortunately, will reinforce my original misunderstanding.

The mechanism through which misunderstandings alter reality is what sociologist Robert Merton (1949) termed *the self-fulfilling prophecy*. The self-fulfilling prophecy is possible because, as a famous sociological axiom states, situations that are perceived as real are real in their consequences. That is, our responses to events are based on our subjective and often biased perceptions and interpretations of what is going on. When incorrect perceptions or interpretations lead to inappropriate responses, those responses nevertheless represent actions to which the other must in turn respond. It is because of this reciprocity that misunderstandings become part of a reality of their own making. As the following example shows, this can happen even among people who know each other intimately.

On the basis of years of experience, Bill was convinced he could tell by her tone of voice when his wife Andrea was angry about something. Arguments often ensued when Bill heard that tone of voice and asked Andrea why she was upset. His steadfast insistence that she was upset while she denied being upset led to numerous heated discussions. In the course of these discussions, Andrea often became upset, which, in Bill's mind, validated his original assessment. Essentially, Bill's perception of Andrea's mood led him to react in such a way as to alter her mood in the direction of his perception. But Bill's self-fulfilling prophecy didn't end here. Because he understood to some extent what was going on, Bill would often keep his perception of Andrea's mood to himself so as not to make her more upset. When Bill talked to me about this, I asked him to describe how he typically would handle the situation if he heard that tone of voice and decided not to confront Andrea about it. He responded that he would usually just leave her alone and hope she would work out whatever was bothering her. He was quick to point out that this rarely seemed to work, however, as Andrea's anger would eventually surface. Each occasion of this sort further reinforced Bill's conviction that he was more in touch with his wife's moods than she was. Was he, or was he creating a self-fulfilling prophecy? Bill's tendency to ignore his wife when he perceived her to be angry was probably based on his admitted desire to be left alone when he was in a bad mood. But Bill also acknowledged that Andrea was a worrier and sometimes kept him awake at night talking about things she was concerned about. Is it possible that what Bill saw as anger was in some cases Andrea's frustration over not being able to resolve something that was bothering her? If so, his tendency to ignore her when she was worried and perhaps needed someone to talk to might have caused her to become angry. As a result of perceiving her to be angry when instead she might have been worried or anxious, Bill responded in ways that eventually made Andrea angry.

One of the arenas in which the self-fulfilling prophecy has been the most obvious is the classroom. A series of studies has shown the importance of teacher expectations on students' academic performance. In a classic study of this phenomenon, social psychologists Robert Rosenthal and Lenore Jacobson (1968) tested students at a San Francisco grade school and then provided teachers with a list of students who they claimed, on the basis of the test scores, could be expected to spurt ahead during the year. Teachers were instructed to watch the students' progress but not report the results to the students or their parents. At the end of the year, students who had been identified as likely "spurters" had indeed increased their IQ scores by ten to fifteen points more than their classmates. The results of this study are dramatic because the "spurter" group in fact had shown no more potential for rapid advancement than other students, for they had been chosen completely at random for that group by the researchers. The only real explanation for their superior achievement during the year was their teachers' expectations.

Unfortunately, it also works the other way around—negative expectations tend to lower student performance. Considerable research shows that poor academic performance makes the student develop negative attitudes toward school, which in turn leads to a host of behavioral problems both inside and outside of school. Most children start out wanting to do well in school, but for a variety of reasons—including teacher and parent expectations—many do not. The frustrations growing out of a failure to keep up in the early years of school often produce aggressive responses that subsequently lead to the child being labeled a troublemaker by classmates, teachers, and school administrators. Children who are given this label are more likely to be placed in lower tracks, where teachers expect poor performance. They are also less likely to be encouraged or allowed to participate in extracurricular activities that keep them busy and teach them valuable social skills. Thus the self-fulfilling prophecy sets up some children for failure and turns them into troublemakers. By failing to understanding this process and the motives behind early disruptive acts, parents, teachers, and other students react in ways that limit opportunities for such children to develop into successful adults.

The self-fulfilling prophecy is most likely to manifest itself in relationships in which one individual is especially sensitive to the perceptions of the other. In parent–child relationships, for example, children tend to base their sense of self-worth on their parents' expressed judgments of them. If parents make a clear distinction between their displeasure with the child and their displeasure with the child's behavior, the parent sets up expectations for more positive behavior in the future. Comments such as "You are a good boy, but you did a bad thing" are preferable to "You are a bad boy," because "bad boys" are often bad whereas "good boys" only rarely do bad things. As suggested earlier, the same principles apply to adults in a variety of situations.

"I Could Have Died . . .": Emotional Reactions to Misunderstandings

Responses to misunderstood acts usually produce additional misunderstandings that ultimately create an emotionally unpleasant situation. The two emotions most often associated with misunderstandings are embarrassment and shame. Although embarrassment is somewhat less personally traumatic than shame, it is nevertheless an unpleasant experience. According to sociologist Erving Goffman (1956), embarrassment is the result of the awareness that our public image has been discredited. Goffman argues that consciously or unconsciously, when in the presence of others we wish to project an image of ourselves that they will view positively. Embarrassment occurs as a result of events that discredit our projected image. Andre Modigliani (1968) suggests that embarrassment also involves a temporary loss in self-esteem; we become embarrassed by events that make us feel bad about ourselves. Fortunately, embarrassment is a temporary state.

Unfortunately, however, it is not a feeling that we can easily hide from others because it manifests itself in two easily recognizable symptoms: blushing and what Arnold Buss calls the "silly smile."

Misunderstandings often lead to embarrassment by creating situations in which we are made to appear conspicuously inappropriate or incompetent. Recall the clerk–customer misunderstanding described at the beginning of this chapter. As a result of mishearing the clerk's statement, "That will be seven sixty-five, please," the customer acted in a way that discredited her status as a competent shopper. The clerk's response to her mistake made her realize that the positive status she had enjoyed only a moment earlier had suddenly become discredited. This led her to blush with embarrassment and quickly flee the situation.

The customer became embarrassed because her misunderstanding led her to act in a way that appeared incompetent. However, we also can become embarrassed as a result of perfectly appropriate actions being misunderstood. Suppose you are shopping, and upon being told that the price of your merchandise is seven sixty-five you correctly repeat that amount to the clerk in order to verify what you have heard. Suppose, however, that the clerk misunderstands what you have said and instead of responding "yes" or "that's right," she says, "No, it's seven sixty-five." Although you have correctly understood the clerk and accurately repeated the price she quoted, she misunderstands you and acts as though you are the one who made the mistake. In addition to feeling somewhat frustrated and perhaps a bit angry, most of us also would feel slightly embarrassed in this situation. Any time our public image is discredited, even though we may have done nothing to deserve it, we feel at least slightly embarrassed because we appear incompetent or inappropriate in the eyes of someone else.

The perception of competence is especially important to those in positions of power. The following is a *Washington Post* article that was reprinted in the *Dallas Morning News* on June 18, 1994.

WASHINGTON—The Clinton administration Friday disowned statements by Jimmy Carter in North Korea, saying the former president evidently had misstated U.S. policy despite earlier consultations between Carter and officials in Washington.

In an embarrassing split, administration officials said that they could not explain why Mr. Carter said in North Korea that the United States had dropped its recent proposal for sanctions against the country, a day after President Clinton had said the diplomatic drive for sanctions would continue.

Because former President Carter was an unofficial yet high-profile representative of the United States government, his statements to the North Koreans were taken as an indication of U.S. policy. Unfortunately, because

Carter's statement contradicted one President Clinton had made the day before, the Clinton administration was made to appear confused about its own foreign policy. In the conduct of foreign policy, often such internal confusion is taken as a sign of incompetence. Fortunately for most of us, our most embarrassing moments are much less public.

Embarrassment tends to be restricted to a particular situation. It is the result of perceived inappropriate or incompetent actions or performances in specific situational settings. Inasmuch as we are all occasionally guilty of inappropriateness or incompetence, such performances are not necessarily seen as indications of character flaws. When they are seen as reflecting personal flaws, however, the emotional reaction is much stronger and longer lasting than simple embarrassment. Failures in situational *performances* produce embarrassment; failures of *character* produce shame. The shamed individual shows many of the same symptoms as the embarrassed individual, although the effects are more pronounced and more lasting. The embarrassed individual might wish to avoid the gaze of others until the feeling of embarrassment passes, but the shamed individual will often attempt to permanently avoid anyone who has witnessed his or her disgrace.

When misunderstandings are seen as a product of who we are rather than what we do, our reaction is likely to be one of shame. Shame involves a feeling of self-disgust, and the loss in self-esteem associated with it is considerably greater than that associated with embarrassment. According to Arnold Buss, shame is the result of a sense of failure, or of actions that we perceive as immoral, antisocial, or disappointing. How can something as innocent as a misunderstanding produce shame? Psychiatrist Donald Nathanson (1992) argues that shame produces a sense that others see us as defective, regardless of what others might really think. The importance of the other is also emphasized by sociologist Charles H. Cooley (1902), who says that what we believe about others influences whether or not we feel shamed in their presence. For example, we would feel more ashamed of displaying ignorance in the presence of someone we consider wise, or of appearing afraid in the presence of someone we consider brave. Thus, regardless of what we have done or not done, if misunderstandings lead us to believe that others judge us as being somehow defective, we are likely to experience a sense of shame.

Aaron Beck and colleagues (1979:179) report the following exchange between a therapist (T) and a patient (P) who was depressed and was ashamed to admit it to colleagues at work. The authors point out that patients don't readily admit to feeling shame, and indeed in this exchange it is the therapist who uses the word *shame*.

P: *If the people at work found out I was depressed they would think badly of me.*

UNDERSTANDING

> T: *Over 10 percent of the population is depressed at one time or another. Why is that shameful?*
>
> P: *Other people think people who become depressed are inferior.*

Notice that the patient does not express personal feelings of inferiority over being depressed. Instead, the focus of the patient's shame is on the way others would judge him if they knew of his depression.

Even when it is a failure to live up to our own standards that makes us ashamed, it is often the responses of others that trigger our emotional reactions. The following account was provided by Mark, a male who prides himself on being able to consume relatively large amounts of alcohol without showing any effects.

> *My wife and I were having dinner with some friends recently when I made a wisecrack to our waiter. Taken out of context, the comment might have sounded cruel, but it was intended as an ironic comment and I certainly did not mean it to be offensive. Well, my wife apparently didn't see the irony and was taken aback by my comment. She suggested that maybe I had had too much to drink. I suddenly felt embarrassed and somewhat ashamed, even though I didn't really feel that I had done anything wrong. I became flustered and snapped back, criticizing my wife for not seeing the obvious irony in what I had said. She said that she was only kidding. I realized that I had overreacted and felt even more embarrassed and somewhat ashamed of myself. Although we smoothed things over pretty quickly, we both felt pretty rotten, realizing that we had each hurt the other's feelings and probably made our friends feel awkward.*

Embarrassment and shame are both forms of social anxiety, and like all forms of social anxiety, they share an acute awareness of oneself as a social object. Recall that one of the primary differences between actors and observers is the tendency of actors to focus on environmental events while observers are focused on the actions of the actor. When we become embarrassed or ashamed our focus turns inward and we become less aware of the environmental cues that help us formulate appropriate responses to events. When Mark became embarrassed because his wife and perhaps his friends had misunderstood his ironic comment to the waiter, he became so focused on his own embarrassment that he might have failed to notice subtle cues that his wife was teasing him. Thus it is a sometimes tragic irony that feelings of embarrassment or shame increase the chances that we will act in ways that will produce further embarrassment or shame.

Both embarrassment and shame are self-perpetuating. We become embarrassed about appearing embarrassed, and knowing that our shame has been made public makes us feel even more ashamed. Each of these emotions is accompanied by an intense awareness of ourselves as public objects. Self-focus can become so intense that we forget what we are doing. This can be a serious problem if we become embarrassed or shamed while we are holding center stage, for example, while giving a public talk or performance. By becoming too focused on how we appear rather than what we are doing, we can become confused or lost, which can adversely affect our performance. I have a musician friend who occasionally forgets the words to one of the many songs he performs. This is obviously embarrassing, as everyone's attention becomes focused on his mistake rather than the song he is singing. I have noticed that he can more quickly recall the words if he makes a public acknowledgment that he is in trouble. Once he acknowledges it, usually in a humorous way, he almost immediately remembers the words and is back on course. Public acknowledgment of something as obvious as embarrassment can help break the tension that comes from intense self-focused attention. A simple honest admission of our dilemma is often all it takes to break the negative trance and at the same time inspire some supportive sympathy from the audience. Acknowledging embarrassment, however, does not mean dwelling on it. The sooner we can return to our original course of action, the quicker the embarrassing moment will pass.

Using Misunderstandings to Make Sense of Things

Although such emotions as shame and embarrassment might be brought on by misunderstandings, the emotions often linger long after the misunderstandings have been resolved. Moreover, in trying to cope with emotionally charged misunderstandings, people are likely to act in ways that lead to further social anxiety. How do we deal with the emotional aftermath of misunderstandings in such a way as to avoid spoiling the entire occasion, creating lasting conflicts, and perhaps damaging interpersonal relationships? Sociologists have identified a variety of strategies, referred to generally as *aligning actions,* which people use to manage problems that arise during face-to-face interaction. Aligning actions include such strategies as (1) expressing an acceptable motive for questionable actions, (2) providing acceptable excuses and justifications, or (3) simply apologizing. These tactics and a number of others allow us to short-circuit conflicts by providing acceptable explanations for problematic behavior.

The use of aligning actions works fairly smoothly as long as we agree on whose behavior requires alignment and who is in the appropriate position to call for and honor or reject alignment efforts. Generally speaking, being in a position of authority is assumed to endow certain individuals with the right to call the behavior of others into account. Parents, for example, may demand that their dependent children explain or justify their behavior in virtually all areas of life. Interaction among equals, however, is considerably more ambiguous, and we often disagree over whose behavior if any should be considered inappropriate. This makes the task of alignment a complex and sometimes risky business. Asking for apologies, explanations, or justifications for behavior can lead to overt conflicts that threaten not only the immediate situation, but also long-term relationships.

Thus aligning actions designed to handle one kind of problem often create problems of their own, not the least of which is that their use requires one person to assume a level of responsibility not shared by others. Even excuses and justifications, which are designed to mitigate admitted responsibility, nevertheless assume that the behavior of one particular actor is responsible for a problem that has become the focus of everyone's attention. Although that behavior might be overtly excused or justified, that does not completely compensate the excused individual for being singled out as a troublemaker.

An alternative and often-employed strategy on such awkward occasions is to explain away problematic behavior and the resulting social discord by *reference to misunderstanding.* Use of the misunderstanding concept in such statements as "You misunderstood me," "Perhaps I misunderstood you," or "I guess it was just a misunderstanding" is clearly an aligning action used to explain away a variety of unacceptable behaviors or interpersonal problems. Elsewhere (Young 1995b) I have referred to such statements as *misunderstanding accounts.* Unlike the articulation of acceptable motives, justifications, excuses, or apologies, misunderstanding accounts require no one to accept sole responsibility for the problems at hand. In fact, the essence of misunderstanding accounts is that they constitute a covert agreement between two or more individuals to overtly share such responsibility. Thus the attribution of problems to a misunderstanding represents a unique solution in that (1) no one is required to deny his or her own perceptions in favor of the other's, (2) no one is required to assume sole responsibility for the immediate problem, (3) interpersonal relationships at least temporarily are salvaged, and (4) everyone is allowed to resume normal interaction.

Below I present a classification of misunderstanding accounts that I have gleaned from the work of other social scientists, from my own analysis of hundreds of misunderstandings described to me by students and friends over the years, and from newspaper articles in which individuals used the term *misunderstanding* to describe various interpersonal problems. In analyzing examples from these various sources of data, I have identified three general types of problems commonly managed by reference to misunderstanding: *communication disputes, motive disputes,* and *propriety disputes* (Young 1995b).

The first type, *communication disputes,* refers to those situations in which the actor and the observer do not share a common view of what the actor has said or done. The communication disputes I have analyzed seem to fall into the general categories of misspeaks (not saying what one intends to say), mishearings (inaccurately hearing what was said), and misinterpretations (interpreting the meaning of an action in a way that is at odds with the intentions of the actor). Thus, perceived communication disputes can result from the action, the perception, or the interpretation stages described above. Miscommunications may produce disputes over such issues as what was said, to whom it was said, what was meant by what was said, whether enough was said, or whether a particular thing was said at all.

A substantial number of student narratives and newspaper articles describe some form of communication dispute. In the following example, a student describes a miscommunication between him and a relative.

> I was involved in a misunderstanding with my brother. The situation dealt with me because I had worked a whole summer in order to pay him for his car, at least what he had asked for it. He wanted six hundred dollars to make minor repairs on it and was practically giving it to me as a gift. Out of the kindness of my heart, I voluntarily gave him an extra one hundred dollars. Eight months later, I still hadn't received the car. So I asked him to return my money and he could keep or sale (sic) the car which would probably benefit him more. He didn't want to do either of the two. He later stated that he was not getting anything from the deal. I misunderstood him from the beginning because I thought he wanted to give the car to me if I paid for the repairing.

A second type of problem that frequently calls forth a misunderstanding account is the *motive dispute*. Motive disputes are the result of different understandings of why a particular action was taken, and can be classified as those involving questions of the causes of actions and those involving questions of the intentions of actions. According to the philosopher John Dewey, motives are not internal states that govern our impulsive responses to various stimuli. They are explanations we use to make sense of observed actions. Reference to motives represents an attempt to place action within an acceptable or at least understandable interpretive context. For example, suppose you are having dinner with someone who refuses a delicious looking dessert. How might you explain this, or, indeed, how would the individual in question explain this? Typically, the explanation would involve a reference to motive, such as "He must be on a diet," or "I've been having trouble with my blood sugar," or "Thank you, but I'm too stuffed to eat another bite." Such stated motives may or may not correspond to the internal states of the person whose behavior is being explained. However, even when we aren't sure why we or others do or don't do things, we often feel compelled to give a reasonable explanation anyway. Thus we attribute motives to others and to ourselves in order to satisfy the need we all have to believe that behavior is rational, or at least understandable. This view of motives is supported by the fact that they only come into question when behavior goes against our expectations. One of the problems with motive talk, as sociologist C. Wright Mills (1940) calls it, is that sometimes we simply cannot agree on which motive makes the most sense. When this happens, we may become engaged in irreconcilable motive disputes. Sometimes these disputes become so acrimonious that they can be put to rest only through the use of a misunderstanding account. The following example of a motive dispute, described by one of my students, is typical.

> *The latest misunderstanding I can remember happened last night in my dorm room. My roommate (also my best friend) was cleaning out her fish tank and I was holding her fish in a plastic bag. At the same time, I was looking through some pictures with my other roommate and kept feeling the fish hitting against the side of the plastic bag. I told my best friend that her fish were having fits wanting back in their tank. When I said it, she was trying her best to get finished cleaning the tank, and took my comment to be criticism. She yelled back at me that she was doing it as fast as she could. She was mad and then I got angry at her, 'cause that isn't how I meant my comment to be taken. We didn't come right out and apologize to each other, but we did try to smooth everything over after it happened. Once she understood, we both more or less forgot about it.*

The motive dispute here is over whether the speaker's comment was intended as a criticism ("You are ignoring your poor fish!") or friendly warning ("Look! Your fish really don't like this."). Moreover, she is not clear as to whether the term *misunderstanding* was actually used at the time of this conflict. Thus we only know for certain that the term was used to minimize the seriousness of the conflict after it had occurred. Whatever account was used on the spot, it was obviously successful since both parties "more or less forgot about it." In contrast, the following example, taken from a newspaper article, illustrates the use of a misunderstanding account to try to resolve an ongoing motive dispute.

> *After the recent funeral for Mr. Brown—who was very popular with teammates— a few players gathered at a bar. Michael was one of them, as were Andre Waters and Wes Hopkins, who were teammates of Mr. Brown's on the Philadelphia Eagles. Mr. Waters and Mr. Hopkins contended that Michael acted boorishly, bragging about his season and a game between the Cowboys and Eagles. "We were there mourning a teammate and a close friend we had lost," Mr. Waters says, "and he was talking about a football game. I didn't understand that. That just goes to show that*

he treasures a football game more than death, and that's wrong. To me, it just showed a lack of respect for Jerome." The incident was a misunderstanding, Michael says: The jovial manner after the funeral was agreed upon beforehand—there had been a no-mourning pact. He, Mr. Brown and a few teammates made the agreement while at a bowl game in college, Michael says. They talked about how they had the best of everything, more than they could have wanted as youths. They would tell each other that when they died, they would "sit right next to God and tell him, 'Thank you, it was great.'" They also agreed to pour a beer on the floor in honor of the departed friend. No one was to cry (Dallas Morning News, January 10, 1993).

In this example, the protagonist, professional football player Michael Irvin, does not deny having acted in a way that might be considered inappropriate, but does deny the meaning attributed to his behavior and, by implication, the presumed motivation for it.

Perhaps the most interesting misunderstanding accounts are those that arise from interpersonal conflicts that seem to involve no actual misunderstanding at all. That is, the term *misunderstanding* is often used to describe situations in which interactants seem to understand each other quite well, but one or both find the other's understanding unacceptable. In the following example, a student uses a misunderstanding account to resolve a *propriety dispute* he is having with a friend.

Recently I was kidding around with one of my fraternity brothers when we had a misunderstanding. I had been drinking and he had been studying in the library. I walked in his room to talk to his roommate, who was not there. He immediately started jumping on my case, telling me I had no reason to be there and I was in violation of quiet hours. I was in no violation of the house rules and became defensive, it turned into an argument, I finally walked out of the room. The next day we both apologized to each other. We found that he had been under a lot of pressure in school and I had been blowing off steam at a bar and at the time our personalities clashed.

Knowing no more than what is provided in the narrative, it appears that the argument that took place between these two students involved no actual interpersonal misunderstanding. Although one or the other might have misunderstood fraternity house rules about quiet hours, they seemed to understand each other's behavior very well, but simply found their wishes and behaviors in conflict. One of the most important aspects of this misunderstanding account is that it provides a temporary identity for both parties that is assumed to explain their clash. In essence, it suggests that a misunderstanding took place between two people suffering from temporarily impaired selves, one due to a lot of pressure from school and the other apparently due to the influence of alcohol.

UNDERSTANDING

Whereas misunderstandings are things that occur between people, misunderstanding accounts are explanations that are constructed by people. Using and allowing others to use such accounts can be a handy strategy for getting out of sticky interactional problems. We should remember, however, that just because someone overtly honors an account, that does not necessarily mean he or she actually believes it. Thus, even when misunderstanding accounts are used to successfully mitigate conflicts, we should not assume that the problems that caused the original conflict actually have been resolved. If we do, we might be surprised to find ourselves in the same predicament some time in the future.

Conclusion: Clearing It Up Doesn't Make It Go Away

In many cases, the first indication we have that our actions have been misinterpreted is when the reactions of the other surprise us. They might seem strange, out of synch, or inappropriate. I have referred to such responses as being *miscoordinated*. If we fail to recognize misunderstanding as the origin of such responses, we can be lured quickly into a spiral of misunderstanding and/or unnecessary conflict. Because inappropriate responses, regardless of their origin, represent serious threats to social interaction, by the time we have reached adulthood, we have developed a repertoire of behavioral strategies for dealing with them. These include ignoring the response in the hope of avoiding conflict or in the hope that further information will help us understand the motives behind the act, and hedging our follow-up actions by giving intentionally ambiguous or noncommittal replies. Because of the ambiguous nature of such responses, however, they can lead to further misunderstanding, and sometimes even create self-fulfilling prophecies. Thus it is occasionally necessary to respond more directly, such as by challenging the action or asking the other for clarification.

Of course, once we become aware of misunderstandings, our behavioral responses often are preceded by a host of emotional reactions that can interfere with our ability to respond effectively. The two emotions most often associated with misunderstanding are embarrassment and shame. Embarrassment is a temporary state induced by an awareness that our public image has been discredited as a result of a flawed or incompetent performance on our part. However, because we are all occasionally guilty of social faux pas, such failings are not necessarily seen as resulting from character flaws. When our actions are attributed to flaws of character rather than performance, however, we experience shame. The loss of self-esteem associated with feelings of shame can be considerably greater than that associated with embarrassment. Unfortunately, because both of these emotions create significant anxiety, they are likely to adversely affect our ability to effectively function and, as a result, can be self-perpetuating. As a result, an honest admission of our feelings is often the only way out of such a predicament.

Finally, it is often possible to use references to misunderstanding as a way of protecting both parties from accepting blame. This sometimes makes it difficult to know when a "real" misunderstanding has occurred and when it has not. However, if any unpleasant interaction can be successfully attributed to a misunderstanding, normal interaction can be resumed with a minimal amount of blame, guilt, or other emotional baggage.

Misunderstanding accounts are typically used to explain potential disputes regarding what was done or said or why it was done or said. In a more strategic sense, however, misunderstanding accounts allow us to lay to rest a variety of conflicts that often can be settled in no other way. Thus, ironically, although misunderstandings often derail social interaction, in some cases it can only be salvaged by an agreement to attribute an interpersonal problem to a misunderstanding. It is thus a tribute to human social ingenuity that we have learned to utilize misunderstandings, which create many interpersonal problems, as a resource for solving others.

PART TWO

MISUNDERSTANDINGS IN CULTURAL AND SOCIAL CONTEXT

CHAPTER **S
E
V
E
N** **7** **Culture Clashes**

*England and America are two countries
divided by a common language.*

GEORGE BERNARD SHAW, *British author*

Whenever they hear the word *culture,* most people think of museums, opera, and Shakespeare. Social scientists take a much broader view of the topic, however. In its broadest sense, culture is composed of all the products of human social life—from Van Gogh to gang graffiti, from Verdi to street corner rap, from Shakespeare to newspaper tabloids. Culture consists of the foods we eat, the clothes we wear, the way we smell, the way we talk, what we talk about, how far away from each other we stand when we talk, and more. In this broad sense of the term, to say that people lack culture is to deny their existence, for to be alive and human is to have culture. Thus, it's not a matter of who has culture and who doesn't, but a matter of which culture shapes our actions and interpretations.

Interpersonal understanding is hampered by the fact that culture doesn't always travel well, either in geographic or social space. What is considered ideal in one place often will be scorned in another. Even in the same place, ideas and actions that pass for legitimate at one point in time will almost inevitably eventually fall out of favor. My students always get a kick out of hearing me describe the first white-collar work clothes I bought when I graduated from college in 1972. They consisted of a bright red blazer with very wide lapels, prominent gold buttons, and a mock belt panel along the backside; brightly colored shirts with very wide collars; large, colorful bow ties; brightly colored plaid, pleated, and cuffed elephant-bell pants; and black-and-white buckle shoes. I have to admit, in terms of fashion, the seventies were outrageous by almost any standard. In fact, looking back, it is hard to imagine how I ever found such a costume attractive. But I did, and so did most other young Americans. It seems reasonable, therefore, to conclude that in another quarter of a century we are likely to look back on today's fashion with similar disbelief.

Although it is one of the most salient products of culture, fashion affects us in insidious ways. When a radical new style of clothing first emerges, most of us are certain that we will never be caught dead in it, and we are able to maintain that illusion for a period of time during which we cast disdaining eyes on those who are crazy enough to actually wear it in public. As the weeks pass and we see movie stars and gradually more and more normal people sporting a particular style, however, we begin to get used to it and eventually begin to think—*maybe.* It usually isn't too long after that that we find ourselves doling out our hard-earned cash for something we once knew we would never want. What is most amazing about this, however, is that when we finally make the fashion plunge, we are not doing it just to keep up with the Joneses, we are doing it because we actually have come to like it!

As humans, we have an inescapable and reciprocal relationship to culture: we create it and it constrains and transforms us. As a result of our interactions with each other, we inevitably produce culture in the form of all the things we create as social beings. But once culture is created, it inevitably influences and constrains how we relate to each other. Like it or not, in one way or another, we are all products of the very culture we help create. Thus, in many ways, what is true of our response to fashion is also true of our response to music, food, or any other cultural products, including each other.

Cultures, Subcultures, and Microcultures

Although culture is all around us, it appears to us as a hodgepodge of sights, sounds, smells, tastes, images, and ideas. Nevertheless, it is possible to think of it in a systematic and organized way. For example, social scientists often make the distinction between *material culture*—including such things as language, music, literature, food, and anything else we can experience with our senses—and *nonmaterial culture,* which consists largely of shared values and beliefs, and the social expectations we have of each other. Although the notion of culture is most often associated with material culture, it is nonmaterial culture in the form of values, beliefs, preferences, and expectations that influences how we perceive and interpret the actions of each other in everyday social interaction. Moreover, it is those subtle and unnoticed cultural habits and orientations that most often create interpersonal misunderstandings.

Because nonmaterial culture is invisible, it is most often problematic when we cross cultural borders. Difficult as it may be, however, we must adjust our expectations whenever we move from one cultural setting to another. Failure to do so makes mutual understanding difficult if not impossible. The following account by a public servant illustrates how difficult such adjustments can be, even when we anticipate the transition.

As a police officer in the city of Dallas I come into contact with a multitude of various racial, ethnic, and lifestyle groups. One particular instance of interpersonal misunderstanding comes to mind. One evening my partner and I were answering a domestic disturbance call involving a family which had just recently emigrated from Mexico. The language barrier was quickly overcome. However, this case involved the husband having physically assaulted the wife for not having dinner prepared properly upon his return from work. Upon our arrival the grandmother and wife quickly attempted to get us to leave the house. We attributed this to the family having come from a very male dominated society. We explained in Spanish that assault among family members is not tolerated in our society (anymore). They continued vigorously to get us to leave, with the grandmother repeating, "No tengo dinero!" We were incredulous. Being white and black male Americans raised in the United States and having learned Spanish in a university, the grandmother's statement was an enigma. It was not until a Hispanic officer arrived on the scene and explained that in some ar-

eas of Mexico the police expect payment for their services that we understood. Once we explained that no payment was necessary nor would be expected, the wife and grandmother were more than happy for us to cart the assaultive husband off to jail.

Obviously, the two police officers who answered this particular domestic disturbance call found themselves thrust into a different cultural world. Despite the fact that they spoke Spanish and had some insight into the culture of the people with whom they were dealing, their cultural knowledge did not extend far enough to overcome a misunderstanding about interpersonal expectations. Such expectations constitute the basic rules of everyday social life. Whether those rules are formalized as laws or take the form of informal habits and conventions, often referred to as *folkways,* they are the basis upon which we create most social interaction.

Precisely because everyday patterns of behavior are culture specific, culture serves the function of binding us to those who share our culture and alienating us from those who do not. Those who are part of the same culture will tend to behave in similar ways and have tastes and preferences similar to each other and at the same time different from those of different cultural backgrounds. Americans like baseball and football, Britons like cricket and soccer; Italians prefer wine, Irish prefer beer; Californians drive convertibles, Texans drive Suburbans. The sum of such seemingly trivial differences can often create cultural gulfs that are difficult and sometimes treacherous to traverse.

But wait. Aren't both Californians and Texans Americans and thus part of the same culture? The answer is both "yes" and "no." Although all Americans are exposed to the same overall culture, we are also a nation comprised of many *subcultures,* or cultural enclaves that share many of the basic elements of the larger culture while maintaining their own unique sets of values, beliefs, symbols, and ways of life. As Americans we share a common language and many cultural experiences, such as the World Series, the Republican National Convention, pizza, and *Seinfeld.* As members of different ethnic, regional, generational, and other subcultures, however, our experiences are incredibly varied. Members of different American subcultures eat different foods, listen to different music, play different games, and often seem to speak different languages—even when they are all speaking English.

Culture exists at an even more intimate level, however. Sociologist Bruce Anderson (1996) uses the term *microculture* to describe the cultural products of small, intimate groups of friends or family members. Children are fond of creating "clubs" with their own secret languages, symbols, and rituals; twins often develop their own language and methods of communication to which even their parents are not privy; and families create their own cultural habits and traditions, which are rarely shared with others.

Culture, therefore, is something we experience at three levels: the macrocultural, the subcultural, and the microcultural. Because culture exists at different levels, we are often required to interact in a number of different cultural contexts in the course of a single day, and we often find it difficult to reacculturate ourselves when we move from one setting to another. For example, the male construction worker who is exposed to a macho all-male culture during the workday might find it difficult and stressful to suddenly become a sensitive and caring husband and father in the evenings.

By adhering to the rules of one cultural community, we often find ourselves in violation of the expectations of another. Moreover, there seems to be no way of avoiding this problem, for even the most spontaneous and unconscious of our actions is a reflection of learned cultural patterns. Mark Zborowski (1953) notes that such patterns exist even in the way we respond to something as personal as physical pain. Different ethnic groups display different responses to pain, and these responses influence the way individuals are evaluated and treated by medical personnel. Zborowski studied hospitalized patients to whom he referred as "Italian Americans," "Jewish Americans," and "Old Americans" (i.e., white, native-born, largely Protestant Americans who did not identify themselves with any foreign group). Before going into the hospital to observe patients, the researchers were told by doctors and hospital personnel that the Italian and Jewish patients seemed to have a lower pain threshold than patients of Old American stock. Citing evidence that all humans have basically the same physiological pain threshold, Zborowski concludes that the differences in the way various groups relate to pain must be the result of cultural influences. Indeed, his observations reveal several important culturally learned differences in the way the three groups reacted to physical pain.

In contrast to the relatively stoic response of the Old Americans, both Italian and Jewish patients complained about pain considerably more frequently and dramatically. But the outward similarity of the responses of the Italians and Jews masked fundamentally different orientations to the experience. Close observation and in-depth interviews revealed that Italian complaints about pain reflected a concern with immediate discomfort and a desire to seek relief. Italian patients readily accepted pain medicine, and once their pain was relieved, their disposition improved and their outlook became generally positive. The complaints of Jewish patients, however, reflected a concern with the symptomatic meaning of the pain. As a result, they were reluctant to accept pain relief, expressing concern about the temporary nature of the relief and possible side effects of drugs. Moreover, the disposition of Jewish patients did not improve substantially once their pain had subsided because they worried that it would recur as long as the underlying condition had not been cured.

UNDERSTANDING

Although their actions reflected different orientations to pain, the outward responses of the two groups were very similar as long as they remained hospitalized. Their outward behavior diverged dramatically, however, when they returned home from the hospital. Italian men who had moaned and complained freely in the hospital were reluctant to do so at home, where they were expected to act as the strong and confident head of the household. Jewish males, however, complained less about pain in the hospital than at home, where they were more likely to use their pain to control interpersonal relationships within the family.

In contrast, the comparatively stoic response of hospitalized Anglos reflected a generally positive attitude toward the medical profession and a high degree of confidence in the scientific approach to health care. Such patients tended to view themselves as part of a team consisting of themselves, doctors, nurses, and other medical support personnel. As members of a team, they considered it their responsibility to provide objective and detailed reports of the pain they experienced so that other members of the team could make an accurate diagnosis and prescribe effective treatment. The authors note that in each case, patients were acting in accord with the expectations of their own culture.

This study is important in pointing to the importance of culture in influencing human responses to various stimuli, even those that are predominantly biological in origin. It suggests that services of all sorts, even medical care, could be greatly enhanced if those who provide them understood the cultural origins and meanings of the various responses they observe in their patrons.

The Language of Misunderstanding

David, an American college student, was about to have his first breakfast in London, where he had gone for a five-week summer course on British culture and society. He had spent several hours the night before in a neighborhood pub talking and drinking beer with a group of English and American students. While waiting in line for breakfast the next morning, David saw John, an English student he had met and enjoyed talking with the night before. As they exchanged greetings, David said: "I had a really good time last night!" John replied: "Yeah, me too, but after a while I realized that I was getting really pissed." David was stunned; he couldn't imagine what he might have done to irritate his new friend, and he was somewhat confused by John's seeming lack of concern for something that had apparently angered him the night before. A few minutes later, when David expressed his confusion to one of the staff, he was informed that although the slang term *pissed* means angry in American English, in England it means that one has had too much to drink. David was much relieved to know that he had not unwittingly insulted his first English friend. That night they both got "pissed."

If Americans are, in Shaw's words, "divided" from their English cousins over their common language, they are also divided among themselves in the same way. Although television, movies, and other forms of mass media are gradually homogenizing American English, misunderstandings still occur as a result of regional variations in dialect. For example, a traveler in the rural South who asks a waiter: "What kind of sodas do you have?" might be told: "None, we just have iced tea and soft drinks."

Although regional dialects occasionally pose communication problems, more serious misunderstandings often occur between those who speak what is often called Standard American English and those who speak one of a variety of ethnic forms of the language. For example, sociolinguist Joyce Penfield (1989) points out that even when speakers of Chicano English and standard English use the same words to express themselves, differences in intonation and cadence can easily cause misunderstandings. According to Penfield, the use of rises and falls in pitch most clearly distinguish Chicano from standard English. In Standard American English, the use of an especially high-pitched voice often denotes a gushy over-politeness, while such pitches are used in Chicano English to highlight or emphasize certain words. It is, therefore, common for Anglos to perceive insincerity in the talk of a Chicano speaker who is simply trying to emphasize a particular segment of a sentence. Another difference is that in standard English, a rising pitch at the end of a declarative sentence denotes a lack of confidence. Such a statement has the effect of a question. However, in Chicano English a similar pattern is often used to stress the importance of the word or words occurring at the end of the statement. Ironically, because of this difference, it will often be the case that the more Chicano English speakers try to be forceful, the more uncertain they are likely to sound to the speaker of standard English.

Many, perhaps most, speakers of Chicano English are bilingual. Because of the widespread acceptance of English as a universal language, however, most speakers of standard English never learn a second language. Because languages and language use are deeply rooted in the overall cultural experiences of groups of people, different languages reflect not just alternative ways of talking but different life experiences. Those who only speak one language, therefore, often are not aware of the fact that ideas and experiences just don't translate easily from one language to another. Because of this difficulty, talk among bilinguals often involves switching back and forth from one language to the other, depending on the topic of conversation. This can make others uneasy and lead them to jump to paranoid conclusions. Consider the following example provided by an American college student.

When I was a sophomore in college, my roommate was a girl from Mexico City. The first couple of months we got along fine, but near the middle of the semester, we had a falling out. I found it very difficult to hang out in my room with my friends, and it always seemed as though her friends would never leave. They were nice enough people, but it is really difficult to study or do what you want to when other people are always there. The most difficult thing I had to deal with was that they would speak in English until they had something "vital" to share, then they would speak in Spanish. It got to the point where it greatly annoyed me . . .

I have heard similar complaints from numerous American students who have foreign or bilingual friends. These students often feel that their foreign friends use non-English when they want to talk about others in their presence. Although this probably happens occasionally, it is much more common that such switching is related to conversing about culturally specific topics for which English is ill-suited. Some ideas and expressions are very difficult to translate from one language to another.

Most of the cross-cultural language problems I have described so far create misunderstandings because they are so subtle that they allow us to believe we understand things we don't. However, cross-cultural discourse is often characterized by such utter confusion that no one is lulled into the mistaken belief that he or she understands what is going on. Among the most difficult language problems to overcome are those that arise from differences in the very structure of talk. For example, in England and North America, verbal descriptions of events tend to follow chronological order, such as: "After I left work, I stopped by the grocery store. Then I went home, ate a quick snack, and got ready to go out." According to linguist Arpita Mishra (1982), however, Indian and other South Asian speakers of English do not arrange the events of their stories in the same linear way. As a result they will sound disjointed and confused to those accustomed to Western English. Discussion of separate events that were part of the same occasion may be separated by lengthy discussions of events that took place at different places and times. The signal that one is referring back to an event that may have been introduced earlier in the narrative, for example, may be no more than the use of the same pitch or tone of voice that was used earlier when referring to the same event. Such subtle shifts are unlikely to be noticed by Westerners, and if they are noticed, their importance and meaning are not likely to be understood.

Many Chinese speakers of English also employ an unfamiliar narrative structure. Linda Wai Ling Young (1982) suggests that unlike English and many European languages, in which sentences tend to have a subject–predicate structure, Chinese and other Southeast Asian languages include many sentences with a topic–comment structure. For example, an English sentence such as *My dog ate my homework* would be stated in Chinese as

Homework, dog ate. The word *my* is seen as unnecessary, since it would be understood on the basis of the context. According to Young (1982), this topic–comment structure is also used to organize larger chunks of talk. Whole multiple sentence and even multiple paragraph explanations mirror this form. The result of structuring an entire narrative in this way is that considerable time is spent paving the way for what they hope will be an obvious conclusion. The Chinese are concerned that stating one's thesis or conclusion first, and then providing justification for it, which is the typical Western way, allows listeners to tune out much of what the speaker says, and that is especially likely if they disagree with the main thesis. The Chinese style, therefore, is one of gently leading the listener through the argument, one step at a time. Westerners often grow impatient waiting for the punch line as they are forced to listen to an elaborate buildup without knowing where it is leading. In addition to fearing that the Western thesis–explanation structure risks losing the audience prematurely, the Chinese consider it somewhat presumptuous to ask the listener to accept an idea without adequate justification. Western listeners, on the other hand, often perceive Chinese speakers to be beating around the bush and never getting to the point.

The Silence Is Deafening

Muriel Saville-Troike (1985) relates a tragic story of intercultural misunderstanding that occurred several years ago during a period of tension between Greece and Egypt. As Egyptian pilots approached the Greek island of Cyprus, they radioed their intention to land at an air base on the island. Their request was met with silence by Greek air traffic controllers. To the Greeks, silence meant that they were not granting permission to land. However, the Egyptians interpreted the silence as a form of consent. Because of this misunderstanding regarding the meaning of silence, as the Egyptian plane approached the runway, the Greeks fired upon it and several Egyptians were killed.

As discussed in Chapter 2, humans can communicate as powerfully with silence as they can with language, and as the above example shows, the use and meaning of silence in social interaction varies significantly across cultures. As with other cultural norms, rules regarding who is allowed or expected to remain silent in what situations and for how long are learned during childhood socialization. Saville-Troike (1985) contends that children being raised in societies that emphasize individual achievement, such as the United States, are allowed to talk more and in a greater variety of situations than children being socialized into cultures that emphasize family and group achievement.

Even those who become proficient in a second language often continue to adhere to the norms of their native culture when it comes to the use of silence. Navajo speech patterns display a significantly longer period of silence between the asking of a question and the giving of a response than do English speech patterns. Thus, when Navajo speakers converse in English with native English speakers, they tend to hesitate for what English speakers consider long periods of time before answering questions. The result is that English speakers will often repeat or restate their questions or sometimes answer for the Navajo before the Navajo is ready to respond. In such situations, the Navajo is likely to appear unknowledgeable, uncooperative, or evasive to the English speaker, who in turn is likely to be perceived by the Navajo to be pushy and impolite.

In some cultures the use of silence can have the same meaning as the use of noise in other cultures. Recall from the earlier discussion of cultural adaptations to the sick role that hospitalized Italians were found to be much more vocal in response to pain and discomfort than the Old (Protestant) Americans. This is consistent with the general stereotype of Italians as being a vocal, expressive people. On the basis of fieldwork in northern Italy, anthropologist George Saunders (1985) concludes that in that culture, where emotions are readily and frequently vocalized, silence can be an especially effective form of communication. He uses the term *noisy-avoidance style* to describe interaction in which minor—often trivial—irritations that are of no real consequence to the actors are expressed loudly and passionately. On the other hand, this style calls for grim and unrelenting silence in the face of real conflict, which tends to be worked out, if at all, behind the scenes by use of mediators. It is easy to see why, in such a cultural setting, silence has ominous implications.

The Italians stand in stark contrast to the Finns, who have elevated silence to a virtue. Lehtonen and Sajavaara (1985) offer the following Finnish proverbs and sayings as evidence:

> Listen a lot, speak little.
> One word is enough to make a lot of trouble.
> One mouth, two ears.
> A barking dog does not catch a hare.
> A fool speaks a lot, a wise man thinks instead.
> Brevity makes a good psalm.
> One word is as good as nine. (p. 193)

A well-known joke about one particular Finnish ethnic group is that "two Hame brothers were on their way to work in the morning. One says, 'It is here that I lost my knife.' Coming back home in the evening, the other asks, 'Your knife, did you say?'"

Lehtonen and Sajavaara suggest that due to their quiet demeanor, Finns are often misunderstood by others. Because they are hesitant to jump into conversations and can tolerate long periods of silence, they are often perceived as less attractive and unfriendly. One can imagine the difficulty Italians and Finns must have when they are forced to interact.

Italians and Finns represent extremes; more subtle cultural differences in toleration for and meaning attributed to silence, however, separate members of many different cultures. The Japanese, for example, can be quite animated, yet they are also tolerant of silence in certain situations, such as those requiring serious contemplation. Although regional and ethnic differences exist among Americans, in general we tend to be closer to the Italians. In fact, according to Lehtonen and Sajavaara, Americans often use talk not to transmit information but simply to avoid silence.

Does That Mean Yes or No?: Cultural Differences in the Use of Context

Anthropologist Edward Hall (1966) argues that the meaning of an event is derived from two types of information: information about the event itself and information about the surrounding context of the event. For example, we know to interpret sarcastic comments made in the context of friendly banter differently from those made in the heat of an argument. Although the comment carries a certain meaning, that meaning can be modified by the context of its use. People from different cultures tend to give different weight to event and context information. Those from low-context cultures pay less attention to the information around an event and more to the event itself. Those from high-context cultures, however, are more likely to attend to and use information about the setting and actions surrounding an event in interpreting its meaning.

In low-context cultures, such as the United States, Germany, and England, what you see and hear is what you get. Not so in high-context cultures, such as Japan, Greece, and Saudi Arabia, where the same words or gestures often mean very different things in different social settings. In high-context cultures where people tend to be very sensitive to the social context, communication is often implicit and indirect. Many Eastern cultures, such as that of Japan, place great value on maintaining harmony and saving face. It is often not so much the existence of harmony, but its appearance and the avoidance of embarrassment that are important. Criticisms are veiled to such an extent that many Westerners would fail to recognize them. A friend from graduate school once said about his favorite philosophy professor, who was Korean, "The most critical thing he ever says about the work of a student or colleague is, 'I don't really understand the point you are making.' Since everyone knows how smart he is, they know he really does understand; what he really means is, 'I think you are wrong.' So if he ever says he doesn't understand you, you know you're in real trouble."

In contrast, low-context people tend to be explicit and direct in their communication style. Americans, for example, tend to get straight to the point and look directly at the person to whom they are speaking. Being frank, even blunt, is often seen as a sign of honesty. In Japan, however, being frank is likely to be considered rude, and looking directly at another person is often interpreted as a challenge. John Graham and Yoshihiro Sano's (1984) research on Japanese and American meetings reveals that Americans maintain about three times as much eye contact as Japanese. Thus, when Japanese fail to maintain eye contact it should not be read as an indication that they are trying to hide something. They are simply showing proper respect.

According to Japanese business expert Diana Rowland (1993), because of their concern with saving face, the Japanese often use the word *hai* (yes) to show respect and assure the other that they are listening. It does not mean, however, that they agree with or even understand what is being said. Likewise, saying "no" directly is considered an affront to the face of the other. Thus, one must read between the lines and interpret the subtle evasions, apologies, euphemisms, and nonverbal gestures that indicate a lack of interest or agreement. According to Rowland (1993, p. 51), "The sound 'sahh,' drawn out, or the sucking in of air through the teeth usually means difficulty. A hand on the back of the neck can also indicate a problem."

Maintaining harmony and showing proper respect for others also manifests itself in extreme modesty and the extensive use of self-effacing expressions. Public expressions of humility, therefore, should not be taken as indicating a lack of confidence. Indeed, overt expressions of confidence are considered rude. Los Angeles Dodgers baseball pitcher Sadeo Nomo provides an excellent example of such humility. In his first year of playing American baseball, the Japanese star was named the National League Rookie of the Year. Upon hearing of the award, rather than commenting on the ability or hard work that had made him a success, his comments were directed at praising America and major league baseball for giving him the opportunity to play here. Ronald Blum (1995) of the Associated Press quotes Nomo as saying, "I proved to people that America has opportunity. This is not only in Japan. If a young talent, a young prospect, would like to get that chance and opportunity, they are welcome to come and should follow me." Less than a year later he pitched his first no-hitter—something most pitchers never accomplish—and would only comment that the game was a big win for his team, which was in the midst of a heated division championship race. Although this type of humility is sometimes found among American athletes as well, anything less would be considered grossly inappropriate in Japan.

Another difference between high- and low-context people is the amount of information they tend to communicate. High-context people, such as the Japanese, are vigilant collectors of information. They often assume that those around them are equally informed. Thus, filling in details is unnecessary. Low-context people, such as Americans and Germans, however, like to compartmentalize information. They do not assume that the listener knows the context of what is being said. Therefore, detailed explanations with every *i* dotted and every *t* crossed are appreciated. For high-context people, however, detailed explanations are likely to be seen as pedantic or condescending, which make them feel bored and/or insulted for being talked down to.

In part, the low-context style of communication that is common in the United States might be a safer and more effective way of communicating in a culturally diverse nation such as ours. However, in culturally homogeneous societies, such as Japan, where shared understandings can usually be assumed, it is not necessary to be explicit. Because an implicit style is likely to be understood only by those who have carefully studied or have been socialized into a particular culture, misunderstandings among people from different high-context cultures are also inevitable. However, because of their appreciation for and sensitivity to social context, high-context people might find it easier to adapt to foreign ways. If so, this might partially explain the success the Japanese have enjoyed in international business.

The Language of Space

Despite our rich languages, humans are not limited to words in our attempts to communicate with one another. The use of space, for example, is one of the most salient forms of visual communication. Like language, however, our use of space varies across cultures, so any particular use of space might mean very different things in different places. Americans are accustomed to commanding a relatively large amount of personal space. As a result, whenever we see two people sitting or standing closer than the standard social distance, we are likely to infer that their relationship is intimate. Such an assumption would be problematic in many other cultures, however, where social space is much closer than it is here.

Anthropologist Edward Hall (1966) has identified three spatial zones that are used in social interaction. In the United States, the *personal zone* extends from about a foot and a half to four feet from the body. This zone, especially its inner area, is restricted to friends and relatives and is often used to reveal private thoughts and feelings. The *social zone* is used for more impersonal conversation and extends from about four feet to twelve feet from the body. Others who see a conversation being conducted from that distance assume that nothing personal is being conveyed and that they are permitted to join in if they wish. In offices, the social zone is often protected by furniture which is strategically placed to keep patients, clients, students, or subordinates at a safe distance. Beyond twelve feet is what Hall defines as the *public zone*. This is the zone used for public speaking. The spatial separation of the speaker from the audience conveys the special status held by the speaker.

Hall points out that these distances are not the same in other cultures. Most noticeably, in Latin America and in most of the Middle East, the social zone is much closer than in the United States. Face-to-face conversations between North Americans and individuals from these cultures are often awkward. The North American, who feels uncomfortable with the closeness of the other, will begin to lean back, then slowly retreat as the other gradually pursues. An Iranian friend once jokingly told me, "We Persians don't feel we are communicating unless we are close enough to smell the other person." It is easy to imagine the kinds of misunderstandings that could occur between individuals accustomed to different interaction distances. In such encounters, North Americans and many Europeans are likely to appear unfriendly and distant, while Latin Americans and Middle Easterners are likely to be perceived as pushy or overly intimate. Hoffer and Santos (1977) describe conflict situations that arise between Anglo and Hispanic teenage males as a result of different cultural norms regarding appropriate social distance and touching.

Arguments, fights, and even murders in local bars have started when a Mexican American male begins talking to an Anglo's date (this may occur even where the Anglo and Mexican American know each other well) and using his own appropriate touch system. The Anglo interprets the touching as sexually aggressive, as an attempt to move in on his date, as an obvious slur on his manhood and reacts, sometimes violently. (p. 328)

As you might guess, cultures that observe relatively limited personal space tend also to be cultures where touching is a common form of communication, and those that allow relatively large parcels of personal space tend to be touch-me-not cultures. Roger Axtell (1991) classifies the following as "touch" societies: Middle Eastern countries; Latin countries; Italy, Greece, Spain, and Portugal; Russia; and some Asian countries. The following could be considered "touch-me-not" societies: Japan, the United States and Canada, England, Scandinavia and other Northern European countries, Australia, and Estonia. France, China, Ireland, and India fall somewhere between. In cultures where touching is common, slight pushing and shoving is also acceptable in crowded places. I learned that the hard way several years ago when I was almost crushed by a group of little old ladies trying to get onto a bus in Mexico City.

Cultural differences in the way space is organized can also produce misunderstandings. In Latin societies, where many homes are built behind walls, Americans will often feel excluded and unwelcome. In North America, we feel some cultural pressure to become friendly with those whose homes are adjacent to or near our own. Our concept of "neighbor" includes such privileges and obligations as borrowing and loaning, socializing, and offering various forms of assistance when it is needed. Americans who expect the same relationship with neighbors in France, Mexico, or numerous other countries are setting themselves up for disappointment. For example, according to Carroll (1988), the French feel no obligation to socialize with others who by circumstance just happen to be occupying an adjacent space.

The same holds for relationships of much shorter duration. North Americans often feel obliged to strike up conversations with strangers with whom they are only temporarily sharing space, whether it is someone they are seated by on an airplane or someone they are standing in line with at the grocery store. Inasmuch as the French feel no such obligation, such instant rapport among strangers is much less common in that country. Thus, the American who unsuccessfully attempts to establish temporary camaraderie is likely to conclude that the French are unfriendly, whereas the American is likely to be seen by the other as a "typical American"—loud and aggressive.

Physical and verbal contact are not the only ways to invade the other's private space. Eye contact can be one of the more dramatic forms of territorial encroachment, and here again we find significant cross-cultural variation, with Americans falling somewhere in the middle. Arabs are inclined to establish and maintain strong eye contact, whereas in such countries as Japan, Korea, and Mexico, direct and sustained eye contact is considered rude. Americans, by contrast, are inclined to make direct eye contact, but do not sustain contact for extended periods of time. According to Marjorie Fink Vargas (1986), English and American interactants look at each other more often than do Swedes, but maintain contact for shorter periods.

Given such diversity in the rules of eye contact, it is easy to see how the same behavior could be interpreted as aggressive and intimidating in one culture and shifty and evasive in another. Americans often conclude that the Japanese can't be trusted because "they won't look you in the eye," while Japanese feel that Americans "try to intimidate with their stare." A Middle Eastern acquaintance used to claim quite frequently that an American woman had given him that "come on baby, here it is, come and get it" look. The Americans who heard these comments assumed that he was just a deluded chauvinist pig. It is perhaps more likely, however, that he was reacting to the vast difference between the typical behavior of American women, who feel free to make fleeting eye contact with strangers, and that of the veiled women in his homeland, who are expected to avoid eye contact with strange men.

Knowing local norms regarding eye contact can help prevent misunderstandings, but may not be enough to protect one from occasional embarrassment. An American woman who is the object of male stares in France or Italy might understand that such behavior is neither unusual nor necessarily frowned upon in those cultures, but such knowledge alone will not insulate her from feeling invaded and/or flattered when it happens. Likewise, knowing that cultural norms prohibit such staring in North America and England may not prevent the French or Italian woman from feeling unappreciated by men from those cultures.

The Language of Time

I just finished reading a series of articles in the March/April, 1997 issue of *Utne Reader* about the ever-accelerating pace of contemporary life and efforts by various groups and individuals to slow things down to a more healthy and manageable pace. I had intended to read it for days before I finally found the time. Notice the way I phrased that last sentence: ". . . before I finally *found* the time." We North Americans, like most of our English and Western European friends, conceive of time as a tangible thing that can be controlled—saved, spent, wasted, invested, lost, or found. The truth is that our sense of time as linear, tangible, and scarce, to a large extent, controls us. Our lives are so precisely scheduled and clock oriented that we have become slaves to our own invention, and invention is just what it is. Our view of time is largely an invention of our Western European cultural tradition. Many cultures scattered across the globe see time quite differently.

One such culture survives in North America. The Hopi, a Native American society in Arizona, has a distinctly non-Western conception of time. According to Edward Hall (1966), the Hopi do not see time as a duration or quantity that can be measured; rather, it is the natural process that takes place while living things live out their lives. Because time is not the same for all things and can be altered only by natural circumstances, it is not controllable in the sense that most Americans imagine it. Hall describes the difficulty faced by government bureaucrats who tried to impose such artificial time control over Hopis involved in construction projects. Because the Hopi could not conceive of there being a fixed period of time in which dams, roads, or houses could be built, they did not see the need to try to conform to government-defined construction schedules.

Another Native American culture with a radically different conception of time is the Navajo. In English, verb conjugations are based on time. Actions are necessarily described in terms of when they take place. The Navajo orientation to time is such that verbs are not conjugated on the basis of time. In fact, the tense of a verb is normally not even specified. As anthropologist Harry Hoijer (1964) points out, detailed descriptions of the motion that produces an action are a more central component of their verb structure. The time when an action takes place, however, is usually not considered important enough to stipulate.

Different conceptions of time are not restricted to small, traditional societies, however. Anyone who has conducted business in Latin America has been confronted with what North Americans see as a distinct lack of urgency. What is considered intolerably late in New York or Chicago is considered on time in Mexico City or Buenos Aires. In general, Southern Europeans are also more relaxed about time than are their neighbors to the north and across the Atlantic. Even in the United States, although formal or business time has been pretty much standardized, as one moves from one region to another and one city to another, it is necessary to acclimate oneself to variations in the use of social time. Among the Mormons of Salt Lake City, it is safer to be early than late to a dinner party, whereas in many other cities a half-hour late is not late at all. The point of recognizing cultural differences in what is considered "on time" is simple. It alerts us to be aware of and try to conform to local customs regarding promptness. It also suggests that we should not be automatically insulted if someone is later than we think appropriate.

The sense of urgency mentioned above, which is so typically American, is related to our sense of time duration. Even those cultures that share with us the belief that time measures duration do not necessarily share a sense of what is a long and what is a short duration. For example, Americans still measure their national history in years, whereas Europeans measure theirs in centuries, and many from Eastern nations can measure theirs in millennia. Thus, the American business executive who mentions long-range planning may have in mind a period of five to ten years, while the notion of long-range planning in Japan might refer to a span of time ten times that long. The same holds true with regard to time units of shorter duration. According to Brislin and colleagues (1986), the working unit of time for Euro-Americans is five minutes, whereas Arabs tend to use the fifteen-minute block. By this informal scale, to be forty-five minutes late for a business appointment in Saudi Arabia is the equivalent of being only fifteen minutes late in America or Europe.

International differences that exist at the cultural level have their analogs at the local subcultural level. A few years ago my wife and I were having tile laid in our house. The contractor with whom we were working recommended someone for the job and we readily agreed to hire him. The old floor had been taken up several days earlier, so after spending the interim walking around on bare dusty concrete, we were somewhat eager to have the job completed. After several delays, the job, which should have taken two days to complete, was begun. Two no-shows, several late arrivals, and five days later the job was finally completed. Although the workmanship was superb, by the time the new floor was installed, the unreliability of the workman had nearly driven us crazy. We were told by the contractor, "That's just the way those tile guys are. I could find you another one, but it would be the same story." Even though the tile guy and I are of the same ethnic background, what we were experiencing was a culture clash. For members of many cultures and subcultures, work is something that goes on during certain hours and on certain days. For others, work is a job to be done, a task or tasks to be performed. Whether it gets done today, tomorrow, or next week is not seen as important.

This more relaxed approach to time is part of a more general orientation to time. Hall and Hall (1987) categorize approaches to time as *monochronic* versus *polychronic*. In monochronic cultures, time is highly compartmentalized—tasks are performed one at a time and interruptions are not easily tolerated—and schedules are adhered to rigidly. The United States, Germany, Switzerland, and Scandinavia are dominated by a monochronic orientation. In Latin American, Middle Eastern, and to some extent Southern European countries, things are often handled in a polychronic way. In polychronic cultures, time is characterized by multi-tasking, schedule flexibility, and heavy involvement in social interaction. Thus Americans who are accustomed to being the center of the other's attention when their scheduled time arrives are often frustrated that appointments in polychronic cultures are frequently interrupted, as the individuals with whom they are meeting freely and willingly share their time with others.

The Body Politic: Nonverbal Gestures and Misunderstandings

Humans communicate with virtually every part of their bodies. Although we normally think of communication as being largely verbal, kinesics (body language) expert Ray Birdwhistell (1970) estimates that only 30 to 35 percent of what is communicated in face-to-face interaction is conveyed by words. Regardless of the accuracy of this estimate, it is clear that our facial expressions, hand and arm gestures, posture, use of personal space, and other nonverbal cues provide an abundance of information to the astute observer. Cultural misunderstandings are frequently the result of the fact that not only spoken languages but also gesture and body languages differ across cultures. In an informative and highly readable book on gestures, Roger Axtell (1991) catalogs hundreds of gestures that have different meanings in different cultures. Here, I will only mention those gestures common to the United States that carry different meanings, and are thus most likely to produce misunderstandings if used elsewhere.

THE HEAD

Every feature on the head is used to communicate. One of the most common gestures is the shaking of the head to indicate "no" and the nodding of it to indicate "yes." Although we might tend to imagine this as a universal gesture, it is not. In fact, in Iran, Greece, Turkey, and parts of the former Yugoslavia, it is the opposite. In India, a "yes" can be indicated by a slow rocking of the head from side to side.

THE EYES

According to an Arab saying, "The eyes are the windows to the soul." People everywhere would probably agree that much is communicated by the eyes. However, as mentioned above, the American tendency to look directly into the eyes of the other as a way of expressing that we have nothing to hide will not be appreciated everywhere, especially in certain Asian cultures, such as Japan, Korea, and Thailand, where looking directly into the eyes of another is considered rude and aggressive. In Taiwan and Hong Kong, excessive blinking of the eyes at someone is considered rude. Although winking is not only a way of flirting but also a common way of acknowledging a shared secret in America, winking the eye is almost always considered impolite in Hong Kong. To close one's eyes while another is speaking is considered a sign of boredom in the United States. In Japan, however, it can mean the opposite; Japanese often close their eyes as they concentrate on what they are listening to.

THE EARS

We tend to think of the ears as an important instrument for collecting information rather than transmitting it. It is a common practice, however, to cup our ears to signal that we can't hear and to hold an imaginary telephone to our ear to signal that someone has a phone call. Several years ago, entertainer Carol Burnett was renowned for tugging on her earlobe as a hello signal to family members at the end of her television show. The gesture was popular for a while and is still used by some of her fans. Perhaps the most common American gesture that utilizes the ears is the rotation of a forefinger around the ear to indicate that someone or something is crazy. In Argentina, however, that gesture is used to signal "You have a telephone call."

THE NOSE

Although the nose is used for creating gestures in many societies, Americans have a limited repertoire of nose signals, none of which are likely to be seriously misunderstood elsewhere. Wrinkling the nose may indicate that something smells bad or it can be used as an indication of disgust. On the other hand, one can indicate an appreciation of fresh air or that something smells good by raising one's head and breathing deeply though the nose. Like most other gestures, however, this one can be used ironically.

THE MOUTH AND CHIN

The lips are made for kissing, or so it would seem. With few cultural exceptions, the kiss is a gesture of affection. Who, where, and when kissing is socially acceptable, however, varies considerably. Kissing the other's cheeks or the air beside the cheeks is a common form of greeting in Russia, France, Italy, and parts of the Middle East. For those not accustomed to this practice, it is difficult to know when one is expected to kiss and be kissed. Roger Axtell advises that people who are about to give you a greeting kiss or kisses will signal their intention by gently pulling you toward them as you shake hands. Although public kissing is perhaps common in France and tolerated in the United States, in much of the Asian world, it is considered an intimate sexual act and is thus inappropriate when done in public.

In conjunction with other parts of the mouth, the lips allow us to whistle. Although this auditory gesture can have lots of different meanings, depending on the context, one obvious cultural difference is that in Europe whistling is the functional equivalent of booing in America. In recent years, probably largely as a result of viewing international sporting events on television, Americans have begun to use the whistle in this way.

As discussed in Chapter 5, purely physical actions—such as yawning, raising the arms to stretch, shaking the head to relieve neck tension, or simply fidgeting in a chair—can have significant social consequences if interpreted by others as social actions. Failure to repress a belch will cause public embarrassment in the United States, but in China a hearty burp is considered a compliment to the cook if it follows a meal. The physical act of spitting in public is considered crude and impolite in most places. Thus, it can be and is sometimes used to express disgust or disdain. In parts of China, however, public spitting is not condemned because it is considered an act of personal hygiene. Similarly, blowing one's nose onto the ground is an accepted practice, while blowing into a handkerchief that one then inserts into one's pocket is considered unclean.

Publicly displaying an open mouth or the teeth within is considered rude in many Asian countries. Thus, public yawning is especially discouraged there, as it is in parts of Europe. Although the tongue should also be kept in the mouth in most parts of the world, according to Roger Axtell, in Tibet sticking out one's tongue is a form of greeting. Finally, it might be helpful to know that in England the chin is also referred to as "the pecker." Thus, don't be too chagrined to hear someone described as "listening intently as he stroked his pecker."

THE HANDS, ARMS, AND FEET

The hands and arms are often used in conjunction with other body parts in the creation of several of the gestures discussed above. Arms and hands, usually as an accompaniment to verbal descriptions, also can be used to symbolize length, volume, and distance. In some cultures, as with some individuals in our society, the hands and arms seem to be an extension of the mouth. In Italy, for example, considerable hand and arm gesturing is seen as a natural part of discourse. In others, such as in Japan, excessive gesticulating of this sort is considered impolite. It is easy to find subcultural differences in the use of these appendages. Contrast the relative lack of hand gestures by country music singers with the exuberant use of them by rap singers. Of course, the arms, hands, and fingers can be used to express complex ideas. American Sign Language literally allows people to talk without vocalization.

People from virtually all cultures use the hands to express emotions. In the United States affection may be expressed by a gentle hand on the shoulder or pat on the back, romantic involvement by holding hands, approval by the familiar thumbs up, and hostility by various hand gestures, the most obvious and negative being "the finger," a universally negative gesture that Roger Axtell suggests has been in existence for over 2000 years. When one is traveling abroad, however, it is important to know that these same gestures may have very different meanings elsewhere. The basic differences between touch and touch-me-not cultures were discussed above. In addition, there are numerous culture-specific meanings associated with other uses of the hands. In certain Middle Eastern cultures and in parts of China and Korea, it is not uncommon for male friends to hold hands while walking down the street, a practice that has no sexual connotations whatsoever. The commonly used "thumbs up" gesture, which in the United States signals approval, has strongly negative connotations (more on the order of "up yours") in Australia, Iran, Russia, Nigeria, Sardinia, Ghana, and various other places.

In a variety of cultures, the left hand is associated with such negative meanings that, when in doubt, one is probably safest to avoid using it altogether. For example, because it is used for bodily hygiene, the left hand is considered unclean in much of the Middle East. Thus one should never use the left hand for eating or for initiating a handshake. In much of the Orient as well as the Middle East, passing food or presenting gifts or even business cards should always be done with the right hand. Using the left for such purposes is likely to be considered gauche. It should be acknowledged, however, that Americans also show a preference for the right hand, which is customarily raised when swearing oaths and covering one's heart when pledging allegiance to the flag. We also try to avoid "left-handed compliments."

When communicating with those who do not share our language, there is a natural tendency to use the hands in an attempt to communicate gesturally what we are unable to communicate verbally. As this very brief discussion suggests, however, one must be cautious in the use of such gestures when traveling in other countries. Although it is easy to miscommunicate when struggling with a foreign language, foreign speakers are easily recognized by their accents and slow and awkward speech, and people everywhere tend to be tolerant of errors made by nonnative speakers. Because natives and foreigners cannot always be easily distinguished visually, however, the gestural faux pas is more likely than the verbal one to be misinterpreted as intentionally offensive. Thus the kinds of misunderstandings that result from linguistic mistakes are often more readily excused than those resulting from the misuse of the hands.

Unlike the hands, the feet are rarely used for gesturing. However, it is still possible to send unintended negative messages with the feet. In many Eastern cultures, simply wearing one's shoes into someone's home will cause offense. The common American habit of propping one's feet up on one's desk would be offensive in such societies as Japan, Thailand, and France. In fact, showing the sole of one's shoe in any way whatsoever is considered rude in many parts of the Middle and Far East. There are also cultural rules, although somewhat less strict, regarding whether and how to cross one's legs while sitting and how to position one's feet while standing.

Conclusion: Same Signs, Different Directions

Each of us is a member of multiple cultural communities. The microcultures of family, friendship, and work groups; the subcultures of the social class, regional, and ethnic groups to which we belong; and the larger culture we call America often confront us with contradictory expectations. In order to adhere to the cultural expectations of one group, we find ourselves inevitably running afoul of the expectations of another. Moreover, by relying on the cultural norms of one group to interpret the actions of someone adhering to the norms of another, we are doomed to misunderstanding.

Cultural misunderstandings are often the result of differences in language use of which we are unaware. The same words and gestures in one cultural group can carry different—even opposite—meanings in another group. Speech cadence, intonation, and verb and sentence structure are all sources of intercultural misunderstandings among people who ostensibly speak the same language. Not only what we say and how we say it, but also what we don't say carries cultural meaning. Differences in when and how we use silence can communicate or miscommunicate as dramatically as words and can create extreme discomfort and serious misunderstanding among people of different cultures.

In all cultures, how we interpret both talk and silence depends on the situational context. However, some cultures are more sensitive and responsive to the social context in which interaction takes place than are others. In high-context cultures, many of which are found in the eastern and southern hemispheres, communication tends to be more subtle and indirect, whereas in low-context Western cultures, such as the United States and Germany, interaction tends to be more direct and explicit. As a result, members of high-context cultures often see low-context communicators as brash and offensive, whereas those from low-context cultures tend to perceive high-context communicators as evasive and inauthentic.

Although the correlation is far from perfect, there is also a tendency for high- and low-context cultures to use social space in very different ways. In general, high-context cultures are characterized by the use of a smaller amount of personal space between interactants than is found in low-context cultures. As a result, individuals from "touch-me-not" societies are prone to interpret the actions of members of "touch" societies as implying more intimacy than is intended. On the other hand, interactants from "touch-me-not" cultures may seem distant and unfriendly to their counterparts from "touch" societies. The use of space is but one of many forms of nonverbal behavior that differ dramatically from one culture to another. The same use of eye contact, which is interpreted as an indication of interest and support in one culture, will be interpreted as a sign of aggression in another. In fact, virtually every part of the body is capable of sending nonverbal messages, and the meanings of these messages are highly culture-bound.

Finally, the way people orient themselves to time is determined largely by their culture. Individuals from monochronic cultures tend to seek control over time by compartmentalizing tasks and adhering to strict schedules, whereas those from polychronic cultures tend to be more flexible with their use of time, allowing social interactions to dictate the amount of time spent in a particular situation. Interactions among individuals with different orientations to time are often mutually frustrating and rife with misunderstanding. Those who have a polychronic orientation are likely to perceive the monochronic individual as frenetic, impatient, and unfriendly, while being seen by the other as undisciplined and irresponsible. It is easy to see why attempts to do business with members of cultures that have a different approach to time can be frustrating and sometimes futile. Of course, each of these cultural differences can be found to a lesser extent within the same culture. In the United States, for example, differences in the use of social space, time, body language, talk, and silence interfere with successful communication across ethnic, class, gender, and regional subcultures.

These difficulties are exacerbated by the tendency of individuals from all cultures to see differences between other cultures and their own as a reflection of the superiority of their own culture. Whether referring to macroculture, subculture, or microculture, social scientists use the term *ethnocentrism* to describe an orientation characterized by the belief that one's own culture is superior to that of others. This orientation discourages one from trying to understand other cultures from the native perspective. It inhibits not only appreciation of but also adaptation to other cultures. It is responsible for the stereotype of the ugly American, the lazy Latin American, and many others. Expecting other people, who come from and live in completely different worlds, to think and act as though they were a part of our world is not only naive, it is unreasonable. This does not mean that when we travel to other cultures, we must "go native" in order to get along, nor does it mean that when we encounter strangers in our own land, we cannot expect some accommodation on their part. It does mean, however, that we must open our minds to the ideas, values, orientations, and lifestyles of other cultures if we are to understand and be understood by those who do not share our own. In an increasingly multicultural world, there is simply no other choice.

CHAPTER 8 Class Acts

Social Class and

Misunderstandings

*The history of all hitherto existing society
is the history of class struggles.*

KARL MARX AND FRIEDRICH ENGELS,
German political philosophers

Several observers of American culture have remarked that in essence we are a society that is integrated from eight to five Monday through Friday, and segregated all the rest of the time. This observation of course refers to racial and ethnic segregation, but it could be applied with equal validity to social class divisions. Most people don't feel especially comfortable interacting with people outside their own social and ethnic group. When individuals from various class and ethnic groups come together for a social occasion, notice the way they distribute themselves spatially. One of the most obvious patterns is that people of the same ethnicity will tend to congregate together. Within those ethnically homogeneous clusters, further spatial segregation is marked by social class. When the occasion that precipitates their contact concludes, they are likely to head home to neighborhoods that remain remarkably segregated. Except for the highly structured setting of the workplace, social interaction across race, ethnic, and class lines is rare. It is rare because all people seem to enjoy most being around people they perceive to be similar to themselves. Unfortunately, because they rarely interact with each other informally, members of different groups don't get to know and understand each other, which reinforces their mutual desire to remain apart. Given their inexperience with each other, it is not surprising that members of different class and ethnic groups frequently misunderstand each other when they do interact.

This and the following chapter will focus on the influence of social class and race on interpersonal misunderstandings. It is important to note at the outset, however, that the reason Americans of different ethnicities and social classes act and react to each other differently is because of differences in culture. Poor people, rich people, black people, and white people are not different because of their incomes or skin colors; they are different because the color of their skin or the amount of income and education they have situate them in different segments of a highly stratified social system. The conditions of their everyday lives have led them to develop distinct cultures as a way of adapting to their social environment. These cultures are then passed on from one generation to the next. Thus, much of what could be said in the next two chapters was covered in the preceding discussion of culture, and readers are encouraged to refer back to some of the issues discussed in that chapter as they read this one.

Why Can't They Be More Like Us? Social Class and Lifestyle

Other than gender and race, perhaps the most recognizable characteristic of people is their social class. It is evident by the way they dress, fix their hair, walk, talk, and gesture. Class is not only recognizable, but it also influences how we live, how long we live, and how we are likely to die.

Despite the importance of social class in American society, many Americans are inclined to deny the existence of distinct social classes and have a pronounced tendency to identify themselves, regardless of their objective class standing, as middle class. Social scientists tend to define class as some combination of education, occupation, and income, but, according to Paul Fussell (1983), author of a witty book on the subject, people's beliefs about what constitutes social class largely depend on their own class standing. Those at the bottom of the class structure tend to equate class with the amount of money one has. Those in the middle tend to see it as a combination of the kind of work one does and how much money and education one has. Those at the top, however, tend to define class in terms of values, taste, style, and ideas. Regardless of how we define ourselves or others in terms of social class, however, the habits, values, attitudes, and lifestyles that constitute social class seem to lock us into rigid ways of seeing the world that interfere with our ability to understand those who are different from us.

People from different social classes frequently make fun of and stereotype each other and rarely stop to think about why they are so different. Consider the following examples. An upper-middle-class man stops by the grocery store on the way home and finds himself standing behind a sweaty man dressed in dirty and somewhat shabby clothes. He leaves thinking that poor people are just dirty and unkempt by nature. He doesn't stop to think that lower class jobs tend to be dirty jobs and that he too would look a bit grimy if he were on his way home from such a job, rather than from his white-collar office job. He doesn't stop to think that lower class children are often dirtier than his kids because they spend more time playing outside, and that they spend more time outside because they live in small, cramped houses or apartments in which they have no space of their own. It doesn't occur to him that his kids stay cleaner because they have their own rooms in which to play, and when they go out into the yard to play, it is covered with a nice layer of well-groomed grass rather than dirt. It is not that he is completely ignorant of these facts, it is just that he doesn't often stop to consider them. He sees some working-class men buying beer and talking about partying on a Wednesday night and thinks to himself: "No wonder they can never get ahead; they are too busy living it up today to think about the future." He can't understand what it might be like to live in a world in which hard work and deferred gratification do not always pay off. Outside the same grocery store, a working-class teen notices a well-dressed middle-aged woman cross the street in order to avoid walking by him. He thinks to himself, "Stuck-up snob! Does she think she is too good to share the sidewalk with me? What is she afraid of? I'm not going to hurt her." He doesn't stop to think that she is not reacting to him personally, but is simply reacting to the widespread image of poor teen-aged males (especially if they are of an ethnic minority) as being the most dangerous creatures in our society. She might not think he is dangerous, but why take the risk?

Such events occur often and everywhere. Failure to understand people of different social classes than our own leads to fear, distrust, and resentment. Although these negative feelings are often unjustified, they are rooted in easily observed differences in the way different groups of people live. What is important to remember is that many of those differences are the result of socialization—the process through which we learn ways of behaving and pass on those ways from one generation to the next. One of the most important things we learn through socialization is language. Although written language is a vital form of communication in advanced societies, the most important tool for sharing ideas and developing mutual understanding among individuals is the spoken word. It is largely through talk that we share our view of the world and come to see the world through the eyes of others. It is also through differences in the way we express ourselves verbally that many misunderstandings arise and persist. Each social class has its own vocabulary, accent, and style of talking, all of which bind members of the same class and simultaneously alienate them from members of other classes.

Talking Class

One of the most obvious ways in which we acknowledge our social class is the way we talk about ourselves and others. Mitchell Brody (1980) has compiled what he calls a "thesaurus of rank" in which he lists *superiority* and *inferiority* words used to describe the same action, thing, or state of being. For example, we are likely to describe a falsehood told by someone of a superior status as an "inaccuracy," whereas falsehoods told by individuals of inferior status are called "lies." A businessman of high social rank who acts ambitiously is "aggressive," but those of lower social rank who act the same way are described as "presumptuous" or "pushy." The upper-class man who is large in stature is "imposing," a middle-class man is "large," and a working-class man is "hulking." An upper-class "lady" has "discriminating taste," and a middle-class lady is "tasteful," whereas a working-class woman is "picky." The upper classes are sometimes guilty of "misjudgments," whereas the lower classes make "mistakes"; the upper classes "secure financing," but the lower classes "incur debt"; the upper classes sometimes "intervene," but the working classes "interfere"; the upper classes are "gracious," and the lower classes are "polite." Of course, these are not absolute rules of speech, but they do represent tendencies people of all classes have to use more flowery and magnanimous language when referring to those of high status and more common and condescending language in talking about those of low status. Notice that not all the terms used to describe the lower classes are pejorative, but even positive terms often have a subtly diminishing quality—such as "polite" versus "gracious." We talk of children as being polite, but rarely use the word *gracious* to describe them. One can easily imagine the "gracious" aristocratic lady giving instructions to her always "polite" maid.

Differences in the way we talk to and about people of different social standing are also reflected in forms of address. Roger Brown (1965) describes what he refers to as the "invariant norm of address" as the tendency to use a familiar form—such as a first name only—when addressing someone of lower status or an intimate of equal status, whereas a more formal form of address—such as a title followed by a last name—is reserved for those of higher status or for equals with whom we are not intimate. Consider the following narrative supplied by a middle-class white male.

> *Shortly after her daughter and I were married, my mother-in-law informed her maid, whom I had known for several years on a first-name basis, to start calling me "Mr. Anderson." She didn't seem bothered by it, but it bothered me considerably, so when I realized that she would no longer call me "Carl," I began to call her "Ms. Williams." Both my mother-in-law and her maid were from the old school, so neither felt comfortable with her calling me "Carl," once I was an adult member of the family. I would have preferred to stay on a first-name basis with her, but I guess my white middle-class guilt just wouldn't let me live with such an inequity, so we now call each other by our last names.*

Inequalities in forms of address are all around us. Gardeners, janitors, and blue-collar workers are casually referred to by their first names by those of higher social standing, who are in turn referred to as Mr., Mrs., Miss, Ms., Dr., and so forth, and many people of all social classes would feel very uncomfortable doing it any other way. Of course, high-status individuals will often use formal address in return as a way of avoiding intimacy with those of lower rank. Changes in form of address from more to less formal often occur when relationships reach a more intimate level. High-status individuals are not inclined to welcome such changes, however, for acts of intimacy between those of high and low status tends to exert pressure toward the equalization of their statuses. The fear of losing status, and thus control, is a powerful motivation for keeping things on a more formal basis. College students, especially graduate students, are often uncertain about how to refer to their professors. Professors who want more intimacy with their students often ask to be called by their first names, and those who want to avoid intimacy insist on being addressed more formally and often use "Mr." or "Ms." in addressing their students. I have learned that assuring students that I don't really care whether they call me "Dr. Young" or "Bob" unfortunately just adds to the uncertainty for many of them. Believing that learning to handle ambiguity is part of becoming a successful professional, however, I have not yet felt compelled to make a more declarative statement on the issue. What is very clear, however, is that in all such relationships the option of becoming more familiar rests with the person of higher status. This too is a very powerful informal norm. The worker who becomes too familiar with the boss, the student who becomes too familiar with the teacher, or the child who becomes too familiar with an adult can count on being rebuked, often in dramatic fashion. But the high-status individual who wishes to become more familiar with the other feels quite free to suggest that they call each other by their first names.

Those who fail to abide by the appropriate norms of address run the risk of being misunderstood. Regardless of the implicit messages they have received from others, lower status individuals who refer to those of higher status by their first names before being asked to do so are likely to be seen as presumptuous. On the other hand, efforts to increase intimacy initiated by the individual of higher status often will be met with skepticism by the lower status individual, who fears being taken advantage of. Because lower status individuals are unlikely to openly express such fear, however, higher status individuals are less likely to realize that they have been misunderstood.

When people of vastly different social class standings do interact informally, differences in the way they use language are also likely to create misunderstandings. Learning the norms of verbal interaction is an important part of socialization, and here we find major differences in the way children from different social classes are taught to interact verbally. Peggy Miller's (1986) observation of mother–daughter interactions in a white, working-class community reveals that mothers use verbal teasing as a way of teaching their infant daughters how to stand up for themselves when they venture out into the world. Teasing is often accompanied by physically combative play, which encourages these girls to be both physically and verbally aggressive. Lower and working-class childhood is tough and children must learn to be tough and aggressive in order to survive. While these lessons serve children well when interacting with others of their own social class, this tough, loud style is often misunderstood by middle-class teachers, schoolmates, and their schoolmates' parents, who see lower class children as antisocial troublemakers.

In lower class families, defiant language is an important part of play. Children who have been teased by parents or other adults are encouraged to defend themselves and defy the authority of the aggressive adult. This is in stark contrast with the more cooperative and mutually respectful style of parent–child play among the middle and upper classes. In both cases, there is an interesting contrast in tolerance for children's defiance in play as opposed to more serious situations. The results of studies such as Miller's and survey results from a national sample of adults (Davis and Smith 1972–1991) reveal an interesting pattern. Middle-class parents tend to be less tolerant of play defiance and more tolerant of serious defiance from their children, whereas lower and working-class parents tend to be more tolerant of play defiance and less tolerant of serious defiance. It is easy to see how such dramatic differences can lead to misunderstandings when children from different social class backgrounds interact. The working-class child's aggressive play is likely to be misunderstood as serious by both children and adults from middle-class backgrounds. Middle-class children who refuse or do not know how to play in this manner might appear unfriendly or "stuck up" to working-class children. In serious situations, however, working-class parents will appear authoritarian and middle-class parents will appear overly permissive.

Not only what we say but how we say it is dramatically influenced by our social class. Social psychologist Michael Argyle (1994) cites research revealing seven significant class differences in speech. When compared to speech of the middle-class, working-class speech

1. *has less complex sentences*
2. *has shorter sentences*
3. *has a smaller vocabulary, less varied adjectives*
4. *has more personal pronouns and adverbs*
5. *is less abstract, more concrete*
6. *takes less account of the different perspectives of listeners*
7. *includes more tags, such as "didn't I?" and "you know."*

It has been suggested that the inclination of working-class speakers to use more concrete and personal accounts, which often fail to adequately take into consideration the different perspectives of listeners, is rooted in the infrequency with which working-class workers are required to converse with people who are very different from themselves. Middle-class workers often must give instructions to subordinates, whose class standing is lower than their own, and at the same time follow the orders of superiors, whose class standing is higher than their own. Thus, they must learn to accurately take the role of a diversity of others in conversations. By contrast, lower level workers receive instructions from above, but are typically required to talk only to those of similar rank. If verbal role-taking is an underdeveloped skill among working-class speakers, it follows that they will often be misunderstood when communicating with people different from themselves.

Of course, people from different social classes will often alter their speech patterns somewhat to accommodate the social class of those to whom they are talking. Such accommodation takes the form of shifting one's accent and speech patterns to imitate or approximate those of the other. There is danger in accommodating too much, however. According to Argyle, people appreciate a certain amount of imitative accommodation, but if the imitation goes too far, it might be interpreted as mocking and considered an insult.

Learning to imitate and otherwise accommodate the speech and mannerisms of those of higher status is one of the tickets to social mobility in our society. Thus, it is not surprising that studies show people from all social classes to be very aware of the class standing of others and able to guess, with amazing accuracy, the class of speakers simply by hearing them speak a few words or phrases. Assuming one has something to say, being able to speak like someone of a higher class means being able to occasionally *pass* for a member of that class, which may open doors of opportunity for real upward social mobility. Of course, real social mobility creates real changes in people, not just in the way they talk, but in terms of the basic attitudes and values they express through their talk. Attitude and value similarity are in many ways at the heart of interpersonal understanding. Social mobility from working-class background to middle-class adult status is the traditional American dream, but the insightful work of writers like Richard Sennett and Jonathan Cobb (1972) suggests that realizing that dream is not always a source of contentment and self-fulfillment. And, more importantly for our purposes, it sometimes creates misunderstandings with those who are left behind.

According to Sennett and Cobb, the price of moving up in the world is leaving behind that part of the world one has grown up with and feels the most emotional attachment to. For many, it also means moving into a life with which one is less familiar and comfortable. Many individuals try to cope with this dilemma by working and living in a middle-class world while maintaining emotional attachment and personal contact with the working-class world they left behind. Despite their attempts to maintain contact with their old working-class friends and family members, they usually find that their old relationships are never the same. One of Sennett and Cobb's informants describes the nature of this dilemma in his own life shortly after he became interested in mechanical drafting in trade school.

Yeah, you can hang out with the guys and have a good time—you know, who got laid last night, talk about that sort of thing—but that's cause everyone can get laid.

*But...when I started to hit the books they sort of didn't feel comfortable with me...
I mean I was the same, I still liked to bullshit about getting laid, I just didn't want to
stay in this lousy place driving a truck or something...so, I don't know, that made me
kind of nervous, 'cause most of the guys have to stay right here...so...I think they
kind of deserted me, but maybe they think I did that...I mean, deserted them.
(pp. 104–105)*

Michael Grimes and Joan Morris' study of sociologists from working-class backgrounds who had earned Ph.D. degrees reveals similar strains. The next two narratives are from their study (for more information about their research, see Grimes and Morris 1997):

*This tension (strained relationships with friends and relatives) arises from the fact
that most of my family does not understand what it is I do. When I first tried to explain to my mother about what I was she complained that I was a "socialist" and
that such politics were unpatriotic. She worries that I will never "settle down and get
a job." My aunt described me to her neighbor as a "schoolteacher." My father told a
friend of his that I was a "babysitter" (this was when I was doing participant observation at a day care facility to collect data for my dissertation). One cousin, when I
detailed some of my activities to her, responded that I was some sort of "professor-
type person."...The rest of the family views me as sort of a mystery member: they
don't know exactly what it is that I do, but they know that it isn't illegal so it must be
OK. I don't think they are afraid of me; they seem suspicious of me though.*

With the possible exception of medicine and law, occupations that require advanced degrees are often mysterious to the general public, especially to lower and working-class people. Although professionals from working-class backgrounds are often proud of their accomplishments, their pride is often tempered by feelings of discomfort and even guilt about the gulf their education has created between themselves and their families of origin. They feel that they can't really be themselves around their own loved ones, for fear that revealing who they have become will make others feel uncomfortable or inferior. Another of Grimes and Morris' (1997) respondents described this dilemma.

*I bite my tongue a lot. I don't want to be seen as a snobby professor type. I can imag-
ine them saying that "she's too good to be seen with us now." I try not to talk about
my work. Although sometimes I find that trying as well, as everyone around me has
no qualms about relating aspects of their own work lives to others. I find it unfair
and frustrating...They must see me as a dreadfully dull person.*

Thus, it appears that by virtue of realizing their parents' dreams of upward mobility, highly educated professionals from working-class back-

UNDERSTANDING

grounds often feel insincere in their interactions with people for whom they care very deeply. They can become so obsessed with avoiding being misunderstood or seen as intellectual snobs that they are willing to accept substitute stigmas, such as being awkward or boring.

Class, Power, and the Problem of Interpretation

In Chapter 5 I introduced the idea that many misunderstandings are the result of one person either over- or underinterpreting the actions of another. I suggested that individuals who have less interpersonal power in a situation will be motivated to closely monitor the actions of the more powerful person because superior–subordinate interactions are usually more consequential for the less powerful person. It follows that this is especially true of interactions between individuals of different social class standings, with the result that misunderstandings due to over- or underinterpretation as well as misunderstandings of substance are more likely. Sennett and Cobb (1972) contend that one of the sources of indignity experienced by working-class people in face-to-face interaction with more educated and "refined" people is the feeling of being judged and the fear of being seen as inadequate. These feelings are exacerbated by the fact that such encounters typically take place on middle-class turf. Situations of this sort produce a hypersensitivity on the part of the working-class people to their appearance and demeanor. When faced with such a situation, the natural inclination is to avoid it altogether, or, if forced to interact, to keep participation to a minimum. This inactivity is often misinterpreted as a lack of interest or concern about the issue or substance of the encounter rather than a fear of being misunderstood or judged harshly by those of higher status.

An example of this happened to me several years ago, when my oldest child was in elementary school (clearly middle-class turf). The PTA in the public school she attended was dominated by upper-middle-class white parents who often complained about the lack of support they received from minority and working-class parents. The latter often did not avail themselves of the opportunity to meet with their children's teachers and become involved in the school, and middle-class parents interpreted that lack of involvement as a lack of concern about their children's education. What these involved middle-class parents failed to understand was that the symbolic meaning they attached to school was radically different from the meaning of school for the parents of poor children. These middle-class parents typically had fond memories of their school days. School was a place where they had performed well and had been rewarded for it. In contrast, many lower class parents remembered school as a place where they never felt comfortable and often were made to feel inadequate. This difference in orientation was especially evident in parent–teacher interactions. To the middle-class parents, teachers were social equals who were providing a service to them and their children. They, therefore, felt relaxed and confident in speaking to teachers. They appreciated the teacher's role, but felt perfectly justified in offering suggestions or even criticisms of the teacher's performance. Lower and working-class parents, by contrast, were more likely to remember teachers as authority figures who judged them negatively and made them feel inadequate. Even as adults who may have achieved a degree of occupational and financial success—and perhaps made considerably more money than the teachers—they did not consider themselves the teacher's social equal. I suspect that for many of them, simply entering the schoolhouse doors brought back a flood of negative memories and feelings they would rather have forgotten. In fact, given the negative experience formal education was for many of these parents, it is a testament to their dedication to their children that they ever attended school functions!

Conclusion: Injuries, Indignities, and Misunderstandings

Despite the fact that our social class is a major determinant of our life chances and significantly influences the way we think, feel, and act, there is an inclination on the part of Americans to deny its power. After all, in a country where all men and women are equal in the eyes of the law, the social class into which one is born should not be a major impediment to success. But all the evidence suggests that it is. Most people are members of the same social class their entire lives. Perhaps it is because of this disjunction between the cultural myth about social mobility and the reality of it that we are uncomfortable talking about class. Or, perhaps in a country in which the effects of race are so palpable, social class differences just don't seem very important.

However, as we have seen in this chapter, social class influences our interactions with each other and produces misunderstandings in a variety of insidious ways. Take, for example, the largely unconscious way in which we refer to those of lower social class by their first names and those of higher rank by their title and last name, or the way in which we employ superior terms, such as "imposing," to describe those of high status and inferior terms, such as "hulking," to describe those of low social status. On a more conscious level, there is the tendency to act in ways that keep relationships among those of different social classes on a relatively formal level, because informality produces pressure toward status equalization. Not only the way we address each other and talk about each other, but the way we talk to and interact with each other is influenced by social class. Whether children respond to frustration through verbal or physical aggression and whether and under what conditions they are allowed to demonstrate defiance toward adults is related to social class. In addition, lower class children tend to be more aggressive in play, whereas middle-class children tend to be more aggressive and competitive in work, often producing misunderstanding and resentment in both arenas. In the adult world, where verbal interaction predominates, their higher level of education and experience in conversing with people of more varied backgrounds give those of higher social rank a distinct advantage.

One of the most salient factors responsible for misunderstandings between those of different social classes is the power differential that normally exists between them. Regardless of one's social class background, there is a general tendency for those of higher status to underinterpret the actions of those of lower status, whereas those of lower status tend to overinterpret the actions of those above them. Although this problem is the result of power rather than class, social status and power differences tend to mirror class differences. Thus, we are likely to see this same pattern of misunderstanding among people of different social classes, even when neither has any formal power over the other.

Fortunately, although social class background significantly influences opportunities for success, it does not completely determine them. Through hard work, talent, and sometimes luck, many Americans do manage to climb the ladder to success. But escaping one's lower and working-class roots is often a mixed blessing, for moving ahead usually means leaving others behind. Many individuals who experience dramatic social mobility are left feeling somewhat adrift, having lost touch with the world they left behind but not completely comfortable with the one they have found. These individuals find it difficult and awkward communicating with the family and friends around whom they grew up, and the frustration and pain this creates often cannot be shared with their middle-class friends, who do not share their perspective. Thus, ironically, the most consequential misunderstandings related to social class sometimes occur among people who have the greatest mutual interest in understanding each other and among whom such understanding at one time was probably taken for granted.

CHAPTER NINE

9

It's All Black and White

Race and Misunderstandings

A racially integrated community is a chronological term timed from the entrance of the first black family to the exit of the last white family.

SAUL ALINSKY, *American political activist*

In his book *The Content of Our Character,* Shelby Steele (1988:6–7) recounts the following incident.

> *When I was a boy of about twelve, a white friend of mine told me one day that his uncle, who would be arriving the next day for a visit, was a racist. Excited by the prospect of seeing such a man, I spent the following afternoon hanging around the alley behind my friend's house, watching from a distance as this uncle worked on the engine of his Buick. Yes, here was evil and I was compelled to look upon it. And I saw evil in the sharp angle of his elbow as he pumped his wrench to tighten nuts. I saw it in the blade-sharp crease of his chinos, in the pack of Lucky Strikes that threatened to slip from his shirt pocket as he bent, and in the way his concentration seemed to shut out the human world. He worked neatly and efficiently, wiping his hands constantly, and I decided that evil worked like this. I felt a compulsion to have this man look upon me so that I could see evil—so that I could see the face of it. But when he noticed me standing beside his toolbox, he said only, "If you're looking for Bobby, I think he went up to the school to play baseball." He smiled nicely and went back to work. I was stunned for a moment, but realized that evil could be sly as well, could smile when it wanted to trick you.*

Steele believes that whether the man was a racist or not, his need to see evil in him reflected a hidden need to see himself as innocent. His argument is that racial strife is largely about power, but before human beings can pursue power with conviction, they must become convinced that they deserve it, and in order to feel that they are entitled to power, individuals first have to believe in their own innocence, at least in those areas where they wish to possess power. He argues that many black Americans need to see racism in order to feel innocent and thus deserving of the power they seek, whereas many white Americans have an equally strong need to deny the existence of racism in order to feel innocent and thus deserving of the power they have. This struggle for the right to feel innocent is often at the root of misunderstandings between black and white Americans.

Steele's view may be correct, but it is even more clear to me that racial segregation has led to the development of two distinct and often opposing subcultures, and that misunderstandings are largely the result of cultural differences. In order to move toward greater mutual understanding, it is necessary to understand that culture develops as a response to environmental conditions. The different physical, political, economic, and social conditions faced by different groups account almost entirely for the cultural beliefs, values, and practices that evolve. Certainly, political, economic, and social systems are themselves products of culture, but once established, they become part of the environment to which individuals and groups must respond. And, as we have already seen, in responding, people often reinforce that very culture.

Rather than probing the very interesting and complex topic of how cultural differences between black and white Americans have come about, in this chapter I will simply identify some of those differences that are most commonly implicated in the creation of interracial misunderstandings, drawing heavily from the work of Thomas Kochman (1981), who has written extensively on the topic of black and white interaction styles.

Black Power/White Power: People or Positions?

One of the first things to acknowledge is that, because we are still largely a socially segregated society, most interracial interactions take place in the highly structured setting of the workplace. To a certain extent, disputes and misunderstandings are circumscribed by the interactional scripts that are characteristic of such formal settings. Moreover, workplace interactions typically take place within the context of relatively formalized structures of power. Who has the most power is usually not subject to negotiation, but the way people respond to and use power can vary dramatically. Thus, in order to understand many black–white differences, it is necessary to understand the differences in the way these two groups think about power.

Sociologist William Gamson (1968) describes power as the ability to mobilize scarce resources to secure desired ends. Whatever allows one to mobilize such resources becomes a source of power. The two most general sources or forms of power are *authority* and *influence*. Authority represents formal power, which resides in social position (e.g., president, general, superintendent, CEO), whereas influence represents informal power, which is based on the ability of the individual to persuade, cajole, intimidate, or otherwise sway or control the actions of others. In essence, these two forms of power parallel the differences between the black and white perspectives on power. According to Kochman, the white perspective sees the power of position as the most legitimate form of power. For power to be legitimate it must be validated by others, and certain individuals are granted respect because of the positions they occupy. Of course, not all authorities act in ways that justify such respect. One of the primary criteria for retaining respect, according to the white perspective, is the ability of people in positions of power not only to act in ways that produce desired results, but to act in ways that are perceived to be rational and dispassionate.

By contrast, blacks tend to see power as something emanating from within the individual. Those deserving of respect are those who are personally powerful and persuasive, those who demonstrate ability. Relatively little respect is accorded people just because of the positions they occupy. No matter how powerful the position one occupies, respect is something that must be earned through accomplishment, although one may be afforded a certain amount of respect for demonstrating a unique or entertaining style in the performance of tasks. And, according to the black perspective, emotion is recognized as an important source of personal strength and power rather than being viewed as something to be suppressed. Thus the display of emotion is granted more legitimacy, and blacks do not insist on the complete separation of emotion from reason. In fact, those who act rationally but without passion or emotion are often viewed suspiciously.

Obviously, these are rather gross generalizations. Variation among individuals within racial groups is probably greater than the variation between groups with regard to their views on power. However, these differences do seem to characterize the broad cultural views of America's two most contentious racial groups. Moreover, it is not hard to understand how such differences might have developed, since in this society whites have traditionally held more formal power than blacks.

It is easy to see how tensions and misunderstandings could develop between people who see power from such radically different perspectives. Whites, who expect to be treated with a certain amount of deference because of the positions they occupy, might not receive such deference from blacks, who are inclined to grant respect on the basis of individual performance and style but not on the basis of position. On the other hand, blacks in positions of authority might be more likely to incorrectly assume that just because white subordinates don't openly complain, they are satisfied with the way they are being treated, as the following account, offered by one of my students, suggests.

> I worked in a day care this summer. My boss, who was an African American, told me the day before I was to come into work, to come in at 1:30 and to work from 1:30–6:30. The next day I showed up at 1:30 and she said "why are you here so early? We didn't expect you until 2:30!" So I was nice to her up front and said "OK, I'll go home and come back in an hour, but I remember you telling me to come in at 1:30 yesterday, I guess I just misunderstood you."
>
> I was so angry with her for not admitting that she was in the wrong. I wanted to tell her off, but since she was my boss I just kept quiet. She made it such a hassle for me to go all the way home and come back one hour later! I really thought she should have confessed, then let me stay that hour that she had once promised me.

In addition to serving as an example of black–white differences in orientation to power, the example also illustrates the use of reference to misunderstanding to account for a *propriety* dispute. The narrator, a white female, was clearly convinced that her boss was wrong and knew it, but would not admit that she was wrong. Yet, she ostensibly assumed responsibility by saying that she must have misunderstood her supervisor's instruction. Although her account suggests that she did not hold her boss in very high esteem, she showed respect for her position by not overtly contradicting her.

In Your Face: Black and White Styles of Discourse

It is often said that racial differences are the result of the fact that we don't openly communicate with each other and honestly articulate our differences. If we would just get together and talk about our problems, we could resolve them. The experience of many people, however, suggests that talking about racial differences often seems to do more harm than good. This is because we often fail to appreciate the differences in discourse style that characterize black talk and white talk. Although black and white Americans share the English language, the ways that they typically use their language differ in important ways.

One of the most obvious differences between the ways in which blacks and whites communicate is the level of passion they display during discussions. Kochman (1981) suggests that this reflects a difference in their approach to persuasion. According to his analysis, the white style of public debate tends to be relatively low-key, impersonal, dispassionate, and nonthreatening. Whites tend to believe that the truth is something that exists independent of individual perception and is, therefore, something to be discovered through rational discussion. The black style, on the other hand, is high-key, intensely interpersonal, animated, and confrontational. Truth is less a thing to be discovered than it is a perspective that wins out in contests of what Kochman calls "dynamic opposition." Thus, for the same purposes, blacks are inclined to use a style whites see as arguing, whereas whites tend to favor what they consider discussion. Because of these differences, whites often see blacks as irrational, not realizing that the emotion they display is an indication of the strength of their beliefs, rather than a loss of control or rationality. Blacks, on the other hand, are inclined to see whites as insincere because they don't seem to really care about what they are debating, not realizing that whites might feel considerable passion about their ideas but have learned to repress their feelings to avoid antagonisms that might bring debate prematurely to an end. This contrast is echoed in the comment of one of Kochman's respondents that "when blacks are working hard to keep cool, it signals that the chasm between them is getting wider, not smaller" (Kochman 1981:20). For whites also, working to keep cool might indicate a high level of antagonism, but it indicates a commitment to keeping the dialogue alive and channels of communication open as well.

The role of emotion is also reflected in the way blacks and whites take turns in discussions. Whites often wish to make several points while they have the floor. The norm in white debate is thus to allow individuals to make all their points, then to respond to them individually during one turn at talk. The norm of black debate is that each point is subject to immediate debate; anyone is allowed to jump into the discussion at any time. Thus whites, who are inclined to allow others to hold the floor for quite a while before responding, are put off by the tendency of blacks to jump in at any point in order to counter an argument. Whites might think, "I didn't interrupt you, so don't interrupt me," while the attitude of blacks is likely to be, "I will interrupt you, but you should also feel free to interrupt me, although I might not easily give up the floor." During debate, it is not uncommon for those involved to level accusations at each other. No one likes to be accused of something that is not true, but the way we respond to such accusations is often taken by others as an indication of guilt or innocence. Here again, unfortunately, black and white styles come into conflict. Whites are inclined to react with indignation and anger to accusations they consider false. Strong and passionate denials are seen as a sign of innocence. To blacks, however, only the truth hurts. Thus, extreme reactions to accusations indicate to blacks that the accuser has touched a nerve. As a result, they are more inclined to ignore such accusations or hurl counteraccusations rather than appear guilty by becoming overly defensive. Unfortunately, it is those very reactions that whites see as an indication of guilt.

White–black styles also conflict as a result of audience reactions to speakers. In discussing the dynamics of black audiences, Annette Powell Williams (1972) states that white audiences can normally be expected to act courteously—that is, seriously and attentively—toward speakers. But what constitutes courtesy is not the same for whites and blacks. Black audiences, she contends, are characterized by a great deal of activity during a speech. They are more likely to move around in their seats and turn toward and comment to neighbors. Whereas white speakers might interpret this as a show of disrespect, black speakers would interpret such activity as an indication that the audience is involved in what they are saying. The fact that, unlike white audiences, members of a black audience do not fix their eyes on the speaker at all times does not indicate that they are not paying attention. Rather, they are actively checking out the reactions of other members of the audience, which is a clear sign of involvement.

It is easy to see how a typical discussion between blacks and whites—especially if it is characterized by disagreement—is likely to go. Black participants may not trust the accounts given by whites, who appear to be too dispassionate to be sincere or real. Moreover, white reactions to accusations typically will make them look even more guilty in the eyes of blacks. White participants, on the other hand, are likely to see blacks as rude, domineering, and irrational. It is no wonder public discussions between these two groups often break down and result in open hostility. An awareness of these stylistic differences and some preestablished and articulated ground rules that respect each style yet produce some kind of compromise both groups can live with should lead to more productive discussions and debates. Again, I am not suggesting that all blacks and all whites employ these contrasting styles. However, unless we acknowledge that certain stylistic differences do exist at the group level and make efforts to accommodate those differences, interracial communications will continue to be unnecessarily strained.

When the Eyes Do Lie

More personal and intimate communications between whites and blacks are also subject to misunderstandings because of cultural differences. As we saw earlier, the messages we convey with various parts of our bodies are an important part of communication, and perhaps no part of the body is more important than the eyes in conveying subtle but important messages. With our eyes, we can wittingly or unwittingly signal a variety of emotional messages. In their study of racial patterns of eye contact, LaFrance and Mayo (1976) discovered that during conversations white listeners tend to look at the speaker as they listen, whereas they tend to look away from the listener as they talk. With blacks this pattern is reversed—speakers tend to look directly at the listener while they talk, but while listening they tend to turn their gaze away from the speaker. Thus, there is much more mutual gazing when blacks are speaking to whites. Unfortunately, such a sustained gaze is often interpreted as a sign of aggression in black culture. Thus, when white listeners attempt to show respect for the speaker by signaling with their gaze that they are paying attention, black speakers are likely to misinterpret such attention as a sign of aggression and lack of respect. On the other hand, when black listeners look away as a sign of respect for the speaker, white speakers are likely to misinterpret that as a sign of inattention or lack of respect.

According to Duncan (1972), speakers and listeners utilize a variety of complex and context-bound nonverbal signals to manage the exchange of speaking turns during interaction. Eye contact is one such signal used to orchestrate turn taking during conversations. However, the cultural rules governing this are also different for blacks and whites. According to LaFrance and Mayo (1976), when white speakers approach the end of a turn at talk, they will return their gaze toward the listener and pause to signal that they are yielding the floor. This strategy often did not work, however, and the white speaker resorted to asking direct questions to get the other to talk, a strategy that, according to the authors, might appear confrontational. On the other hand, when the white listener encountered a sustained gaze accompanied by a verbal pause from the black speaker, the white misinterpreted that as an invitation to speak, and both found themselves talking at once. Because of such differences in turn-taking signals, whites might often find themselves interrupting black speakers. Although not all whites and blacks adhere rigidly to these patterns, they are probably common enough to produce many awkward moments among interracial interactants. Moreover, because the interactants are not likely to be aware of the cultural differences that produce such moments, they are likely to attribute them to malevolent motives on the part of the other.

Misunderstandings Up Close and Personal

Not only do whites and blacks differ in the way they interact, but what are considered appropriate topics of conversation are also different. Inquiries about personal information, for example, are handled and interpreted somewhat differently by the two groups. According to Kochman (1981), whites who are meeting for the first time often share information about what they do for a living, where they live, what their spouses do, and where their children go to school. Sharing such information is just part of being friendly. Blacks, he contends, are somewhat more reluctant to share such information and consider it prying to ask direct questions about private matters. Information that whites readily share in public blacks consider no one else's business. Thus, they are likely to consider it highly insensitive to directly ask for private information, and those who offer it too freely are often seen as boasting. Kochman attributes this difference in part to the greater importance whites place on social status. They believe that knowing such information helps one better understand the individual. Blacks, however, place less importance on social characteristics and more on personal characteristics, such as charm, intelligence, and wit; these are the things that constitute the real person, and they are revealed in the way people act, not in their social status. This sentiment is expressed in the phrase often heard in music lyrics as well as everyday discourse: "Be for real."

Because many blacks consider asking direct questions to be presumptuous and intrusive, they would prefer to wait until the information is volunteered. When it is deemed necessary to probe, inquiries are likely to be much less direct than in white talk. Questions are asked indirectly by *signifying,* which, among other things, is a way of suggesting more than is actually said. In general, the ability to signify in creative and humorous ways is greatly valued. It can be used for a variety of purposes, including insulting, but it is an especially valuable tool for broaching private and potentially sensitive topics. Moreover, this form of indirect inquiry is not reserved for strangers and distant acquaintances; it is often found in conversations among intimates. Claudia Mitchell-Kernan (1972:323) offers the following example from a conversation between two sisters. Although she has not yet been told, Rochelle either knows or strongly suspects that her sister Grace is pregnant.

> Rochelle: *Girl, you sure need to join the Metrical for lunch bunch.*
> Grace: *(noncommittally) Yeah, I guess I am putting on a little weight.*
> Rochelle: *Now look here, girl, we both standing here soaking wet and you still trying to tell me it ain't raining.*

Because blacks are alert to the use of significations, they are more likely than whites to assume that the direct questions have some implied meaning that may or may not have been intended. Thomas Kochman (1981: 104) reports that he was involved in such a misunderstanding when he asked a black student actor, whom he was watching rehearse, whether it was her first play. Although he was simply seeking information in a typically white (i.e., direct) way, the student interpreted his question as a signification, replying, "Did it look like that up here?" Kochman (1981:104) quotes another example of such a misunderstanding between a television studio technician and a group of black students who were waiting to use the studio.

> White studio technician: *As soon as you've finished eating your sandwiches, we can start taping.*
> Black director: *(jokingly) Oh, that means you want us to get finished eating quick and get our asses in there.*
> White studio technician: *No: if I wanted you to hurry up, I would have said so.*

Distrust, Deception, and Misunderstanding

Although cultural differences in the way blacks and whites converse, react to speakers, and request information can easily lead to unintentional misunderstandings, it would be naive to deny that members of both groups occasionally use deception with the other and intentionally create ambiguity and misunderstanding. In fact, psychologists Joseph White and Thomas Parham (1990) contend that experiences with slavery, Jim Crow legislation, segregation, economic oppression, and racism (both individual and institutional) have made many African Americans distrustful of whites. Distrust begets deception, and black literature and the oral tradition are full of advice to blacks to be cautious about being honest with white people. White and Parham (1990:80) quote from an old slave song:

> Got one mind for white folks to see
> Nother for what I know is me
> He don't know don't know what's on my mind.

According to Grace Sims Holt (1972), through the use of such linguistic devices as *inversion,* blacks have developed a code of meanings that are virtually invisible to whites. Inversion involves using a word or phrase to imply the opposite of its standard usage. Employing words such as *bad* to mean *good* and *nigger* as a complimentary rather than a derogatory referent reinforces solidarity among blacks and obfuscates their meanings to whites. Moreover, the interpretation of inverted words and phrases is dependent on subtle subcultural contextual cues that are often obscure to the outsider. Thus the purpose often is to intentionally create misunderstanding.

Whites, on the other hand, have been the primary authors of various forms of bureaucratic doublespeak, inflated language, and euphemisms also designed to give a false impression. White and Parham (1990:77) quote Stokely Carmichael's response when the white-controlled news media said that President Johnson had a credibility gap in communicating about the Vietnam War. Said Carmichael, "Credibility gap, hell, that honkey is just lying." This statement illustrates both the disdain many blacks have for such euphemisms as *credibility gap* and the lack of respect they grant individuals simply on the basis of the formal power they have.

Woofin,' Dissin,' and Getting Serious—
How Blacks and Whites Handle Conflict

According to Kochman (1981), whites invariably interpret verbal expressions of anger and aggression as more threatening than do blacks. Among whites, expressions of intense anger, especially if coupled with personal insults, are a sure sign of impending violence. Blacks, on the other hand, employ insults and challenges in a variety of different ways, many of which do not signal the initiation of violence. Aggressive talk, often referred to as "woofin'," is a recreational pastime among many lower class black youths. In such groups the trading of insults against foes and/or members of their family, referred to as "rappin'," is a daily ritual. Linguist William Labov (1972) has done expensive analysis of the implicit rules that govern such activities as playing the dozens, a highly ritualized game in which combatants trade insults, most often directed at the other's mother, until one either backs off or becomes violent. For example, one of the implicit rules in rappin' contests is that whether or not an insult is to be taken personally depends on how outrageous it is. Statements that are so outrageous that they could not possibly be true are ritualistic and are not considered genuine insults ("Your mother's so fat, she got confused for the Goodyear blimp"); those that come too close to the truth, however, ("Your mother's so poor, she can't buy groceries") are considered personal rather than ritual insults. Resorting to personal insults or violence is often a sign that one has lost the game. Although such games are normally played only by young lower class males, anyone who grows up in a black community is likely to have at least witnessed such rappin'. Such activities show quite vividly the learned ability of blacks to sustain verbal aggression without resorting to violence. The ability to express one's frustrations and anger without resorting to violence is no doubt an important skill for members of a repressed minority.

The ability of blacks, and the relative inability of whites, to manage and maintain intensely hostile confrontations through verbal devices without resorting to violence reflects an important cultural difference between these two groups. According to Kochman (1981), whites practice self-control through repression. They learn to hold in their emotions, but they don't learn how to manage emotional forces once they have been unleashed. Overt shows of anger and verbal aggression among whites, therefore, suggest that they have lost self-control. Blacks, on the other hand, are much more confident in their ability to verbally vent their emotions without losing control of them. Thus, they are quick to vent their frustration and anger. Given these differences, it is easy to see how the meaning of aggressive verbal exchanges between blacks and whites could be misunderstood, sometimes with disastrous results.

Conclusion: What We Have Here Is a Failure to Communicate

One cannot talk about race relations without talking about power. For a variety of historical and political reasons and because they constitute the numerical majority, whites have always held political and economic power. Thus, all the ways in which power influences the way we perceive each other impedes interracial understanding. Perhaps because of our different experiences with power, blacks and whites have very different attitudes and beliefs about it. In general, it appears that blacks are more inclined to see power as something that resides in the individual, whereas whites tend to see it in terms of the position one occupies. Inevitable conflicts and misunderstandings result from this difference. Because for blacks power must be generated from within, in face-to-face confrontations they are more likely to show intensity and animation in arguing their point, whereas whites tend to be more impersonal and dispassionate. In the face of accusations, however, the trend is reversed, with whites seeing strong and

UNDERSTANDING

passionate denials as a sign of innocence and blacks seeing such displays as a sign of guilt. The way we attend to speakers differs as well. During intimate conversations, white observers tend to fix their gaze on the speaker, whereas blacks tend to focus elsewhere. In communicating their ideas, however, whites tend to avoid direct eye contact with the audience, whereas black speakers seek it. In terms of the content of messages, whites tend to be more direct and explicit and blacks tend to be more indirect and implicit. As a result, blacks are likely to perceive whites as pushy and presumptuous and to be seen by whites as evasive and dishonest. Inasmuch as both groups feel that they have good reasons for doing what they do, both have difficulty understanding why the other behaves so differently.

Because their interests are often perceived to be incompatible, blacks and whites often find themselves embroiled in conflict. Unfortunately, the way they handle conflict is so different that their styles make resolving disputes even more difficult. Whites interpret verbal expressions of anger as more threatening than do blacks. Woofin' and rappin' among blacks are often used as substitutes for physical violence, but whites see such posturing as signaling violent intentions. Because they are often more practiced at it, blacks are able to manage hostile confrontations through such verbal devices to a greater extent than whites, who learn to hold their emotions in check. As a result, whites fear blacks because they see them as hostile, and blacks distrust whites because they see them as cold and uncaring.

Black and white Americans have lived in social isolation, and for most of their history have been residentially, educationally, and occupationally segregated from each other. As a result, they have developed distinctly different cultures. Their language and lifestyles evolved on parallel yet separate courses. Today, institutional segregation no longer exists, yet social segregation persists, and the need for blacks and whites to communicate on a regular basis has not eliminated the many sources of misunderstanding that continue to interfere with their attempts to cooperate in dealing with the complex problems our society faces.

CHAPTER **TEN**

10

She Said,

He Heard

Women, Men, and

Misunderstanding

Men and women, women and men.
It will never work.

ERICA JONG, *American author*

Tommy runs into the house crying. "Daddy, Daddy, Jimmy hit me!" "Well," responds Dad, "get back out there, and if he hits you again, you hit him back."

Annie runs into the house crying. "Daddy, Daddy, Elizabeth hit me!" "There, there, precious," responds Dad, "if she does that again, you let me know and I'll have a talk with her Mommy."

Virtually everyone who survives childhood has memories of events such as these, and with few exceptions the advice given children in this kind of situation depends primarily on the child's gender. Granted, mothers might be less likely than fathers to recommend that their sons hit back, but it is hard to imagine many middle-class American mothers or fathers advising their daughters to do so.

Starting from the Beginning

The worlds of boys and girls are vastly different, and although many people assume that these differences reflect innate differences between the sexes, there is ample evidence that they are largely the result of the ways boys and girls are treated, even from the first moments of life. Observations in hospitals reveal that newborn boys tend to be bounced and jostled around more and generally handled more roughly than girls. Boys are also allowed to cry longer before being picked up and comforted. These differences reflect parental perceptions of newborn boys as being hardier, stronger, and less needy than girl babies. When Rubin, Provenzano, and Luria (1974) asked the parents of newborns to rate their babies on a variety of characteristics, they found that parents of girls described them as softer, smaller, finer featured, less attentive, more awkward, weaker, and more delicate than did the parents of newborn boys. In contrast, parents of boys described their babies as firmer, larger featured, better coordinated, more alert, stronger, and hardier. Independent objective assessments of these babies taken by doctors and nurses, however, revealed no differences between the boys and girls selected for the study. All the described differences, concluded the researchers, were in the eyes of the beholding parents.

In another study, conducted by John and Sandra Condry (1976), 204 adults viewed the same baby on videotape. Half the adults were led to believe they were watching a boy baby while the other half thought they were viewing a girl baby. When asked to describe the baby's reactions to a variety of stimuli, those who thought they were observing a boy described the baby as more active and potent than those who thought they were viewing a girl. When the baby cried, those who thought they were viewing a boy attributed the crying to anger, while those who thought they were viewing a girl attributed it to fear. In a more recent study Dena Ann Vogel and colleagues (1991) found similar results when they asked children from five to fifteen years of age and college students to rate the actions of a videotaped toddler. These studies and many others like them reveal the dramatic differences in the way we perceive and the expectations we have of boys and girls, literally from birth on.

Many of these studies were conducted in the 1970s, a decade in which our society was engaged in a serious and critical look at the opportunities and expectations traditionally associated with one's gender. Significant (though in many cases surprisingly minor) changes in expectations and opportunities for both sexes have taken place since then. However, inasmuch as these studies were done during or after the childhoods of those who are now adults, they reveal a great deal about the way most contemporary adults were reared.

Growing Up and Growing Apart

Early childhood expectations are not without significant consequences. One of the first lessons both girls and boys learn is to be different from each other. Boys learn quite early that the most important lesson in being a boy is *don't act like a girl!* Gender differences that might appear minor in the early years become more pronounced as children grow and begin to interact and play with other children. Daniel Maltz and Ruth Borker (1982) argue that girls and boys grow up in different sociolinguistic cultures, and that the rules for carrying on friendly conversation are very different in these cultures. During the impressionable period from five to fifteen years of age, boys and girls interact primarily with members of their own sex, where they learn to self-consciously differentiate themselves from each other. Studies of school-age children reveal dramatic differences in the way kids play and interact with one another. For example, whereas it is common to see schoolgirls hugging, holding hands, and dancing together, among boys such shows of intimacy are strongly discouraged, even to the point of ridicule. Eder and Hallinan (1978) suggest that rewarding girls and punishing boys for intimate behavior leads girls to value the one-on-one contact they have with best friends, while boys learn to fear it. This influences group interaction in that girls prefer spending time in small groups or with a single best friend, whereas boys are more comfortable interacting and playing in larger groups. This may be one of the reasons boys are more likely than girls to be drawn to organized sports and games.

As a result of such gender-specific play routines, girls and boys learn different lessons. Boys, contends Janet Lever (1978), play more complex games in which they learn to deal with role differentiation, formal rules, and teamwork. They also learn to deal with interpersonal competition in an honest and straightforward way. Girls, on the other hand, by engaging in more spontaneous, imaginative, and less structured activities in smaller groups learn different verbal skills, such as how to recognize subtle emotional cues and how to deal with a greater variety of emotions. As Deborah Tannen (1990) suggests, boys learn to cooperate with teammates in order to win, while girls learn to cooperate with friends in order to maintain relationships. These and many other differences are actively learned and cultivated in childhood. As a result, when men and women try to communicate they are operating by different sets of rules, and the results can be quite confusing.

As psychologist John Gray's (1992) catchy "men-are-from-Mars, women-are-from-Venus" metaphor suggests, by the time men and women become adults, it often appears that they are from different worlds. But what exactly do those early socialization experiences tell boys and girls about being men and women? Much has been written about the nature of the traditional female sex role and the limitations it places on women, but relatively little has been written about what men are supposed to be. Perhaps this is because scientists and scholars tend to study things that are considered problematic. Until recently, the traditional male sex role was largely ignored by scholars precisely because it was not seen as problematic. As Robin Lakoff (1975) points out, traditionally men have been the dominant sex; thus, whatever they were was valued and therefore not considered in need of study. As the more destructive aspects of maleness have been increasingly acknowledged, however, more attention has been given to exactly what the male sex role consists of. Deborah David and Robert Brannon's (1976) book *The Forty-Nine Percent Majority* elaborates the major dimensions of this role. According to these authors, the male sex role is characterized by four major themes. These themes, which boys learn early on and which are reinforced throughout life are (1) *No Sissy Stuff,* (2) *The Big Wheel,* (3) *The Sturdy Oak,* and (4) *Give 'em Hell!*

NO SISSY STUFF

In traditional families fathers spend extended periods of time away from home. Boys spend less time hanging around with and directly observing their fathers than girls spend with their mothers. As a result, boys know less about real men than girls know about real women. Where, then, do boys learn what being a man is about? Unfortunately, they learn it largely from the fictional and fictionalized men of movies, television, and professional sports. Whether they like it or not, these men *are* significant role models for boys. Another source of (mis)information about manhood is other boys. Thus, the blind lead the blind as boys emulate the behaviors of distant characters whose lives bear little in common with those of their fathers and other real men. Not knowing exactly what one is supposed to be like can be difficult, but one of the first lessons all boys learn, according to David and Brannon (1976), is: *Don't be like girls, kid, be like . . . like . . . well, not like girls.* This means above all else, no sissy stuff! The lesson unfortunately leads to exaggerated hypermasculine behavior and severe sanctions against any boy who appears sensitive, weak, or vulnerable. The hidden fear that underlies this message and stifles male friendships, these authors argue, is the fear of being seen as homosexual. This fear strongly discourages boys from sharing the kinds of feelings and information with other boys that are the hallmark of girls' friendships.

THE BIG WHEEL

The second theme associated with the traditional male sex role suggests that real men are those who are successful, who are looked up to, who amount to something. Unfortunately, all men do not succeed by conventional standards, and even those who do succeed often feel like failures despite what others might consider impressive accomplishments. Men who do not succeed in the normally recognized ways often become obsessed with success in other areas. Symbols of success, whether they be a big house, fancy cars, or the loudest stereo system, are seen as critical indicators of manhood. Part of being a big wheel is being competent, and the need to feel competent encroaches on all areas of men's lives. Women often comment that men will speak very authoritatively about things they obviously know nothing about. Admitting you don't know something is anathema to being a big wheel. One of the places men feel intense pressure to show competence is in bed. How else, ask David and Brannon (1976), could we account for the proliferation of sex manuals that provide step-by-step instructions for men on how to satisfy any woman? They quote one wife as saying, "My husband has studied those things so much, I can tell when he is flipping from page forty-one to page forty-two" (p. 22). Also associated with the Big Wheel theme, and a critical measure of whether or not a man feels successful in life, are his accomplishments in the bread-winner role. Real men provide for their families. Thus, it is not surprising that studies of unemployment show that men suffer considerably more emotional and psychological stress as a result of job loss than do women.

THE STURDY OAK

The third theme associated with the traditional male sex role demands that a man always maintain an air of confidence, self-reliance, and toughness. Like a fictional character out of the Old West, a real man is one who can stare danger in the face and not flinch. Being a sturdy oak means being physically and emotionally strong and invulnerable. This, of course, means never acknowledging or talking about one's fears or insecurities, especially around other men. Real men don't complain, and they don't do therapy!

GIVE 'EM HELL!

Whereas the sturdy oak theme demands that a man be strong and independent in the face of hostile forces, the give 'em hell! theme demands that he occasionally become a hostile force. That requires being daring and aggressive, even if it also means occasionally being violent. Calling a man "aggressive," whether one is referring to an athlete, businessman, or professional, is usually considered a compliment. The glorification of aggression and violence among men is legion. From violent movies to violence in sports to a fascination with war, men are supposed to be aggressive, and a certain amount of violence is tolerated, if not revered. Unfortunately, such violence and aggression are not restricted to interactions with other men, as revealed by crime statistics on rape, spousal abuse, and child abuse.

The pressure to live up to the demands of the male sex role and the virtual impossibility of doing so in every respect can lead to obsessive and sometimes unhealthy behaviors. Consider the following example, given to me by an acquaintance.

> *Tom was my first really good friend after I graduated from college, but he was very competitive. Unfortunately, no matter what we did I seemed to be better at it than Tom. Instead of avoiding competitions, however, Tom went out of his way to find new activities at which he could beat me. From sports to women to grades and finally to such trivial pursuits as pinball, Tom was a man obsessed with beating his best friend. Although I'm not all that competitive myself and found all this competition tiresome, I never let Tom win, even though it would have made my life easier if I had. I felt that if I had let Tom win by not doing my best, I would have been disrespecting him.*

This example shows how important such matters as competence and aggressiveness are to men and that even those who do not personally subscribe to such stereotyped notions of manhood tacitly support them in others. Tom's friend never talked to him about his discomfort with their constant competitions. Nor did he ever try an obvious strategy that many women would have probably adopted—he never let him win. When Tom's friend says he never let Tom win because that would not have been giving him proper respect, he meant that by letting him win he would not have been treating him like a man.

At every point, the male sex role described by David and Brannon (1976) stands in direct contrast to the traditional female sex role. Although tomboys are more readily tolerated in our society than effeminate males, girls are strongly encouraged not to be like boys. For girls the message is clearly, *no macho stuff!* If men are supposed to be *big wheels,* women are supposed to be *quiet wheels,* never calling attention to themselves unnecessarily. Whereas men fear failure, women often fear success. Smart girls learn quickly to downplay their intelligence and hide their academic achievements if they want to get dates. If men are supposed to be *sturdy oaks,* women are expected to be *steel magnolias,* able to quietly handle the pressures of everyday life by yielding but not breaking. Handling such pressures means relying on others rather than being completely self-reliant. It also means not being self-centered but being supportive of others, if possible without their knowing it. Finally, assertiveness is tolerated on occasion, but overt aggressiveness is hardly ever considered appropriate female behavior.

Although many parents are raising their children to defy the limitations of these traditional sex roles, those same parents still struggle to overcome their own sex role socialization in an era of greater gender equality. Perhaps in a few generations, many of the gender differences that make male–female communication so problematic today will have disappeared. For now, however, many men and women still find it difficult if not impossible to fathom the mind of the other. However, despite the fact that many men and women are quick to acknowledge their inability to really understand members of the opposite sex, they often fail to recognize how frequently they misunderstand the actions of the other. Confusion, anger, separation, divorce, and outright hatred can be the results of such misunderstandings.

In order to understand each other better, women and men must get a better understanding of some of the basic ways the other sex communicates. Let us start by looking at how and why men and women talk and how their talk differs. First, however, it is important to acknowledge that the differences I will be reporting represent differences in general and will not necessarily hold for all individuals. In fact, some of the characteristics attributed to males will be more characteristic of some females and vice versa. Moreover, many of these differences are most pronounced when interaction takes place in same-sex groups. Thus, it appears that when they interact with one another both women and men try to accommodate themselves—although often without success—to the style of the other. Finally, the existence of differences does not imply that either style is superior to the other, although certain ways of communicating are sometimes interpreted as a sign of greater or lesser status.

Why Men and Women Talk

Even more fundamental than the fact that women and men talk differently is the fact that they often talk for different reasons. Research suggests that women use talk not only to convey information but to establish connection with others and to cope with stress. Men, on the other hand, talk primarily to convey information and to establish, challenge, or maintain status hierarchies within relationships. Numerous studies support these conclusions. As I reported earlier, boys' play groups tend to be highly organized and geared to primarily competitive activities. Cooperation among boys is often for the purpose of winning against another team, but as the composition of teams varies, so do alliances. He who is your friend today might be your enemy tomorrow, and friendship cannot be allowed to get in the way of winning. The phrase, "Nothing personal, just business"—a phrase that is most closely associated with male speakers—clearly reflects this early lesson. Elizabeth Aries (1976, 1987) found that conversations among boys who had just met each other involved numerous references to tricks, practical jokes, and other forms of one-upmanship as they attempted to determine where they stood in relation to each other. A preoccupation with their position in a status hierarchy is behind the ritual fighting, mock insults, and direct challenges so common among both boys and men. In her research on conflicts among preschool playmates, Amy Sheldon (1993) found that boys in conflict are concerned with asserting their positions of dominance in the group. Girls, on the other hand, are more concerned with avoiding conflict. When conflict does erupt among girls, they are also more likely to attempt to negotiate a mutually satisfactory solution. In fact, several different studies suggest that one way for a girl to lose status is to be seen by others as "bossy."

These differences are reflected in the results of an extensive study of middle-school students conducted by Donna Eder, Catherine Evans, and Steven Parker (1995). In the school they studied, the popularity of boys was determined primarily by their athletic ability and participation. The jocks were the most popular boys, and virtually all the boys agreed with and accepted the legitimacy of this ranking. The most popular girls were the cheerleaders and a more extended group of girls they considered their best friends. Moreover, there was a widespread belief among girls that making cheerleader was based on factors other than merit. Thus, the popularity of boys was determined almost solely on the basis of achievement, but the popularity of girls was seen as being dependent upon social ties. Finally, the most popular boys were almost universally liked, whereas the most popular girls were perceived by many other girls as snobs and were disliked by about as many people as were the lowest status girls.

This study helps us understand two important things about how adolescent peer socialization influences interaction patterns in adulthood. First, if being liked by others, which is a primary concern of adolescents, depends on one's social ties, then it makes sense that one would be diligent about establishing and maintaining social relationships. It is not surprising, then, that women learn to nurture friendships and use talk as a way of doing that. For men, however, being the big wheel and getting respect is more important than being liked, and respect is something granted on the basis of perceived achievement. Personal achievement, or at least maintaining the appearance of achievement, is what it is all about. Second, the application of the snob label to popular girls by less popular girls suggests that they are less comfortable than boys with status distinctions, which they tend to minimize whenever possible.

In addition to establishing status, men talk in order to convey information and provide assistance to others. Their talk with each other centers predominantly on sports and work. I have heard many men confide that if it were not for sports, they wouldn't know what to talk with their fathers about. When men have phone conversations with their parents, they might talk briefly with their fathers about work and their favorite sports teams and at length with their mothers about family, friends, and plans for family visits. One middle-aged male who lives quite a distance from his parents and only sees them a couple of times a year reported that when he calls them and his father answers the phone, their conversation often lasts only a few seconds, and goes something like this:

> Son: Dad, how are you?
> Father: Fine, you?
> Son: Pretty good. Did you see the game?
> Father: Yeah, it was a good one.
> Son: Yeah.
> Father: Well, let me get your mother.
> Son: OK, good talking to you.
> Father: Yeah, you too.

Numerous authors point to the reluctance of men to talk openly about problems, especially to other men. Deborah Tannen (1994) believes that this is because men fear that any admission of vulnerability on their part will result in a loss of status and put them in a one-down position with other men. As a result, men often do not talk when they have problems. Instead, according to John Gray, they withdraw from interaction in order to ponder and work on their problems. During these periods they might find it difficult to concentrate on other things and are likely to be essentially noncommunicative. When caring females ask them what is wrong, they are likely to answer that nothing is wrong or that they do not know. What they do know, however, is that they don't want to talk about it until they feel that they understand it and have something informative to say.

Women talk for different reasons. As mentioned before, one of the primary reasons women talk is to establish rapport and connection with others. Unlike men, when they have problems they typically like having someone with whom to talk about it. The phrase *talking it out*, which is an integral part of women's language, is less often heard from men. By engaging in such talk, however, women are not necessarily looking for solutions. They are simply looking for reassurance that they are not alone, that someone else understands and cares. Talking helps them relieve stress. Other women, who understand this, will often respond to such "troubles talk," as Tannen (1996) calls it, by telling sad stories of their own. Unfortunately, instead of offering expressions of sympathy and understanding, men who do not understand this will frequently attempt to minimize the problem, assuring women that things are not really so bad. Rather than being reassured, however, women often feel that such comments indicate that men do not take their problems seriously. Alternatively, or in conjunction with the minimizing strategy, men will attempt to tackle the problem head-on, offering one possible solution after another. Of course, none of their suggestions seems to get anywhere because it is not a solution women are looking for. Thus, what could be occasions for achieving greater intimacy often end up with both parties more frustrated and alienated than ever.

Talk As Cooperation or Competition

Do unto others as you would have them do unto you. A nice idea, but one that assumes that others will interpret your actions as you intend them. Because of differences in the way men and women interpret the same actions, applying the golden rule in cross-gender communication can be problematic. Perhaps a better rule in this domain would be *Understand the other's style and never forget it!*

As numerous authors have pointed out, women's talk tends to be cooperative, supportive, and polite, whereas men's talk tends to be more competitive and individualistic. Much of women's talk is directed not so much toward accomplishing tasks or sharing information as toward establishing rapport and mutual understanding. They do this in a variety of ways. Ruth Bend (1975), for example, studied gender differences in tone of voice among midwesterners and found that women used more variety in tone of voice than men, especially those indicating politeness, surprise, and cheerfulness. One of the more common ways women establish rapport with other women is through what might be called "ritual complaining." Deborah Tannen (1994) points out that women often initiate interactions by issuing complaints. However, these complaints are largely ceremonial, designed to initiate conversation and elicit sympathy from the other. They do not necessarily reflect serious concerns. Men often do not understand the ritual nature of such complaints, however, and feel compelled to offer solutions. As one husband I talked to reported, "Sometimes I'll start showing real concern and trying to find a solution to her problem, and she'll just stop and say, 'Oh, it's OK, I'm just bitching.'" Women are more likely to respond to ritual complaining with a simple and sympathetic response, such as, "I know what you mean" or "I often feel the same way." Having thus established contact and rapport, they might quickly move on to another topic.

Showing concern for and solidarity with the speaker is a significant concern for many women, who employ a number of linguistic devices to assure the speaker of their interest. One such device is the frequent use of such terms as "yeah" and "Um-hum" to indicate that they are paying attention and are interested in what the other is saying. Unfortunately, as Daniel Maltz and Ruth Borker (1982) point out, men often interpret such responses as indications of agreement. The result is that they are often surprised when women subsequently act in ways that are inconsistent with such agreement. Such perceived inconsistency leads them to conclude that one can never tell what women really think. In contrast, men are more likely to sit quietly as they listen, making no response at all. In fact, in some cases, the more attentively he is listening, the less likely he is to respond while the woman is talking. He is allowing her to have her say without interruption. Women, who are looking for signs of interest, however, become convinced that men never listen to them.

Women also frequently interject questions as a way of showing interest. Unfortunately, men often interpret such questions not as signs of interest but as indications of ignorance. Of course, women also ask questions in order to gain information. In fact, Deborah Tannen (1994) contends that they are more likely than men to do so. For example, she contends that when a couple is traveling in their car and realize they are not where they thought they were, men are more reluctant than women to ask for directions. This reluctance is often attributed to the unwillingness of men to admit defeat. However, Tannen (1996) suggests that because men are more likely to espouse knowledge they might not be sure of, they assume that others will do the same. Thus they don't necessarily trust that whoever they get directions from will really know how to get them where they are going. Women, on the other hand, who are believed to be less reluctant to admit that they don't know something, are more trusting of the information they receive from others. The cost of asking questions, however, can sometimes be high. Tannen (1994) reports the story of a female intern who, despite being one of the best interns in her group, received a low grade from the supervising physician. She asked why she had received such a low grade, and was told that it was clear that she didn't know as much as the others. When she inquired as to how he had come to that conclusion, his reply was, "You ask more questions" (p. 26). Although I have not compiled systematic data on this, it is my distinct impression that women students in my classes are more likely than men to ask questions, whereas men are more likely to make comments and express opinions. I have also noticed that women who express controversial opinions are more likely to be criticized by other students, both males and females, than men who express such sentiments.

Asking questions and interjecting supporting utterances sometimes interrupt the speaker, although they are used primarily to indicate interest. Other forms of interruption are more obtrusive, such as butting in to take over a conversation. Studies of interruption show that men and women interrupt in different ways. Although women are more likely to interrupt in the more supportive ways just described, men are more likely to interrupt in order to make assertive comments or change the subject of conversation. Don Zimmerman and Candice West (1975) analyzed conversations from both private residences and public places. They found that the great majority of all interruptions that occurred in male–female conversations were men interrupting women. Since then, a number of studies have replicated their results, some of which also have found interruptions more common in all-male conversations than in all-female conversations. Others, however, have suggested that many overlapping comments—those made while another is speaking—are not really interruptions, but constitute side comments. An example of such a side comment would be asking a dinner companion, while she was talking, if she would like more water. Clearly, interruptions can be used to take control of a conversation, enter into it, or express support for the speaker, and how an interruption is interpreted often depends on the individuals involved.

Given the patterns of socialization discussed earlier, it is clear that in interaction with their peers, boys adopt a more assertive approach to conversation than do girls. Therefore, it is not surprising to find that men are more likely than women to interrupt speakers. However, Bohn and Stutman (1983) found that men were also more likely to interrupt each other than women were. Men not only interrupt but are also frequently interrupted by other men. The conversational rule among men seems to be, *I'll interrupt you when I want to because I know that you will do the same.* The rule among women seems to be, *I won't interrupt you, so please don't interrupt me.* Obviously, these rules conflict when women and men talk with each other.

One of the most dramatic cases of aggressive interruption among males occurs during story-telling segments. Maltz and Borker (1982) cite several studies of storytelling among boys that reveal the competitive nature of all-male conversations. These studies consistently show that boys who tell jokes or stories to other boys cannot expect an attentive, cooperative audience. In these groups, the speaker is frequently interrupted, mocked, and challenged. In order to get through the joke, he must be able to successfully fend off challenges to practically anything he asserts. If he is unsuccessful, he must yield the floor to more aggressive orators, thus losing status. Girls' and women's story-telling style is much more cooperative. They are less inclined to tell formal jokes and stories in which a speaker narrates the entire episode without inviting the participation of others. Mary Crawford (1995) describes the female style as one in which the speaker states a main point and recounts the remainder of the narrative with the cooperation and encouragement of others. Again, interruptions among girls and women tend to be more cooperative and facilitative, whereas those employed by boys and men appear to be more competitive and disruptive. Although the female style is likely to be seen as more polite, even by males, if that style were used in some male groups it would probably be interpreted by speakers as indicating a lack of interest and involvement on the part of the audience.

As much of the previous discussion suggests, women's talk appears to be more polite and less assertive than men's talk. Borrowing a term from the chapter on cultural misunderstanding, women's talk is more *implicit,* whereas men are inclined to make more *explicit* assertions. This orientation leads women to be more indirect in their communications. A husband might say, "I'm hungry, let's eat," whereas a wife would be more likely to take a less direct tack by asking, "Are you hungry?" According to Robin Lakoff (1975), women have evolved a more indirect style of speech because of their subordinate position in society. Such a style, she argues, serves two functions. First, it allows the speaker to disclaim a particular meaning if the listener reacts negatively to the comment. Second, by communicating without making demands or exercising power, the speaker establishes emotional closeness and rapport with the listener.

A common form of indirect speech is the use of *tag questions,* which Lakoff describes as halfway between an assertive statement and a yes–no question. For example, an utterance such as *The party is starting too late, don't you think?* expresses an opinion, but in doing so it invites the opinion of the other. Failing to appreciate the rapport-maintaining function of tag questions, men often interpret them as indicating uncertainty. However, other authors disagree with Lakoff's characterization of the implication of tag questions. Women, according to Tannen (1994), are more likely than men to ask the opinions of others in order to get a sense of what others think before making a decision. Simply as part of trying to understand others, women are often interested in knowing their opinions, even if they have already made a decision. Cameron, McAlinden, and O'Leary (1988) go even further in arguing that tag questions often function not to mitigate but to augment the force of a comment by controlling the response of the other.

Tannen (1994) argues that men use indirection more than some authors have recognized. However, she contends that men and women are indirect in different situations. Women are indirect when they are trying to get others to do things; men are indirect when expressing personal vulnerabilities or worries. Moreover, she contends that indirection need not be associated with a lack of power, as Lakoff (1975) suggests. Imagine an employer saying to an employee, "It's cold in here." The astute employee, realizing the implication, would not hesitate to ask the employer if she would like the heat turned up. On the other hand, such a comment on the part of the employee might safely be ignored by the employer, thus necessitating a more direct request, such as, "Would you mind if I turned up the heat?" The ability to move others to act simply by making indirect suggestions is surely a sign of power, albeit disguised and thus in a feminine form.

Another linguistic device employed most often by women, according to Lakoff (1975), is what I will call *declarative questions*—statements made with the intonation used in asking a question. Such statements are often used to make an assertion without appearing too assertive. For example, if a woman says, "I'll see you tomorrow at ten?" is she asserting that she expects to see the listener at ten o'clock or is she asking whether ten o'clock is an acceptable meeting time? Perhaps both, but by using such declarative questions, women are likely to be seen as less sure of themselves than the man who declares, "I'll see you tomorrow at ten."

People often employ nonverbal gestures and acts in place of more direct verbal requests or demands. If women are more inclined to be indirect, they are probably more sensitive to indirect suggestions by others. My wife and I have an ongoing, although mostly playful, battle over laundry issues. One issue is my tendency to remove clothes from the dryer and pile them on the bed with the intent of folding them later. Often, however, my wife will see them and take it upon herself to fold them before I get around to it. After this happened several times, I discovered that she thought my piling them on the bed was a subtle request that she fold them. The gender difference was revealed the first time she left a pile of clean clothes on the bed. When I did not follow her lead by folding the clothes she had placed there, she confessed that she had hoped I would take the hint. Admittedly, in both cases, our conflicting styles led to more work on her part. In some couples, one partner simply feels greater urgency to get certain things done than the other. This partner will thus be the first to take the initiative to do the work, often assuming incorrectly that the other has been waiting for him or her to do it. This partner is unlikely to be convinced by such assurances as "I would have gotten around to it."

What's So Funny? On Gender and Humor

According to Regina Barreca (1996), author of *The Penguin Book of Women's Humor,* Liz Carpenter wrote a book about her experiences in Washington after serving in the White House during the Johnson administration. Some time after the book was published she ran into Arthur Schlesinger, Jr. at a cocktail party. When he saw her, he approached and jokingly quipped, "I liked your book, Liz. Who wrote it for you?" Carpenter quickly fired back, "I'm glad you liked it, Arthur. Who read it to you?"

Despite such improvisational abilities, women are often viewed as lacking a sense of humor. Joanne Cantor (1976) used the Liz Carpenter anecdote to test people's perception of women's and men's sense of humor. She constructed a similar story and used two versions of it. The first version read:

> A movie actor, soon after his autobiography was published, was approached at a party by an actress, who said, "I saw your new book ... Who wrote it for you?" "I'm so glad you enjoyed it," came the reply, "Who read it to you?" (166)

The second version was identical except that in it a movie actress was the author and the person issuing the insult was a male actor. Half of the subjects read the first version and half the second version. Subjects were then asked to rate how funny the story was. Cantor discovered that both men and women rated the first version as significantly funnier than the second. She then repeated the experiment by using two other versions of the story. In the first, a female actor insults another female actor; in the second, a male actor insults another male actor. In this version of the study, both men and women rated the female/female story as significantly more funny than the male/male version. Cantor's conclusion: regardless of who does the ridiculing, people find it funnier to watch a female ridiculed than to see a male ridiculed.

This may be in part because people are more accustomed to seeing women ridiculed for the sake of humor. Mary Crawford (1995) points out that there are entire categories of jokes about women for which there are no male equivalents—for example, prostitute jokes, mother-in-law jokes, dumb-blonde jokes, women-driver jokes, and Jewish-mother jokes. This tendency to make women the butt of jokes is not solely the work of men, however. One need only watch the routines of female stand-up comedians to be struck with the number of such routines involving the comedian making jokes about her own body or other personal deficiencies. On the other hand, in mixed-sex groups, especially in work settings, women are frequently exposed to off-color humor, which they find offensive and not very funny. If they laugh they are indirectly contributing to their own degradation, but if they don't laugh, contends Crawford (1995), they are accused of not having a sense of humor.

Crawford and Gressley (1991) argue that men's sense of humor is not better or worse than women's, but that it is simply different. In order to study such differences, they asked respondents to think about the funniest person they knew. They then had them describe that person and what made that person funny. Their results revealed that both men and women consider creativity the most important dimension of a good sense of humor. For women, however, it appears more important that a person use that sense of humor to benefit others—for example, by using humor to cheer up someone. Although Crawford and Gressley had too few respondents to allow them to draw definitive conclusions on this point, their results suggest that men are more tolerant of hostile humor than are women. The kind of hostile bantering that is common in all-male groups is rare among women, and male comedians such as Don Rickles, whose humor centers almost exclusively on insulting others, have no successful parallels among women.

Deborah Tannen (1994) also contends that women and men are attracted to and practice different types of humor. Women create humor out of discussions of life events and relationships; they tell humorous real-life stories in which the entire group participates. In contrast, men seem to enjoy telling jokes, a form that allows the speaker to hold the floor as others listen. They also are more likely to generate humor out of the immediate situation. These sessions often involve making fun of one another and bantering back and forth.

Recent studies have demonstrated a link between laughter and both mental and physical health. Humor is an important element in human interaction. Whether or not people can come to really appreciate what others find humorous, understanding that gender and other cultural factors influence our own and others' sense of humor might at least help us avoid turning humor into humiliation and conflict.

Queen of the Hill: The Power of Words

Because of women's traditionally subordinate position, suggests Robin Lakoff (1990), people have tended to see anything associated with women as inferior. Even their communication style has been devalued simply because it is different from men's style. As evidence for this assertion, she points to the research of Jacques Ellul (1965) on Malagasy conversational practices. Malagasy men speak indirectly and evasively, whereas women speak directly and to the point. This is, of course, the opposite of male and female styles in our society. Although the gendered styles of talk found in these two societies are opposite of each other, there is one thing they share—a devaluation of the female style. Whereas in our society the more direct style employed by males is considered honest and trustworthy, in Madagascar that same style is seen as an indication that women don't know how to converse properly and logically. Because women are assumed to be inferior, asserts Lakoff, their language is assumed to be inferior, regardless of the form it takes.

Of course, language is only one area in which women's performance is devalued. In many occupations women still receive less pay for doing the same work as men. Philip Goldberg (1975) set out to test the idea that antifeminine bias distorts perceptions of women's competence. In order to study this, he asked college students to critically evaluate six different articles on a variety of topics, ostensibly to test the students' critical reading abilities. The reported sex of the authors, which was randomly assigned, was revealed by having their names prominently displayed at the head of the article. Goldberg discovered that when an article appeared to have been written by a female author, it was given significantly lower ratings than when the same article was attributed to a male. Although this finding did not especially surprise the researcher, two other results did. First, men were not alone in giving lower ratings to articles attributed to female authors; women also showed a marked prejudice against women authors. Second, these results held not only for articles on such topics as business and law—areas traditionally associated with males—but they also held when the articles were on such traditionally female topics as elementary school teaching and dietetics. Thus, both men and women devalued work they associated with female authors, even in areas in which women are normally believed to have special expertise. Although Goldberg's study does not link the devaluation of women's work to language style, it does show that women often have more difficulty than men in eliciting appreciation for their contributions. The devaluation of women's language is just part of a larger problem. Because of the prevailing power structure, however, to the extent that women's language differs from that of men, it may put them at a disadvantage.

Conclusion: When Difference Is Disadvantage

The fundamental differences in men's and women's ways of talking are summarized nicely by Deborah Tannen (1994), who concludes that women often put themselves in a one-down position and expect others to come down with them, whereas men put themselves in a one-up position and expect others to boost themselves up. This certainly seems to be the essence of many of the differences discussed above. As Tannen, Lakoff, and other writers have shown, women's language, in subtle ways, often serves to undermine their status in the eyes of others, especially in the eyes of men, whose style is more aggressive and self-promoting. By asking questions and seeking opinions, women run the risk of appearing less intelligent and decisive. By being indirect, they run the risk of appearing uncertain. By saying they are sorry as a way of showing sympathy, they may be seen as assuming responsibility. In attempting to soften the blow of criticism by tempering it with a compliment, they run the risk of not having their criticism taken seriously. By employing troubles talk to establish solidarity, they might be inaccurately perceived as chronic complainers or as needy.

One conclusion to be drawn from this discussion is that women should try to change the way they talk so that they talk more like men. As Lakoff (1975) points out, however, women are essentially damned if they do and damned if they don't, for those who adopt a more masculine style of interaction are criticized for being unfeminine. Women who adopt this style are often seen as threatening both to men, who fear being replaced, and to other women, who fear falling behind more assertive women. At the same time, men's style of interaction has served them well, at least in terms of meeting instrumental ends. Thus, it is unlikely that they will dramatically change their style in the direction of women's language. What is more likely is that we will see both cultural assimilation and accommodation. That is, as women continue to make inroads into traditionally male domains, these two styles of talking and interacting will increasingly merge. In this process, let us hope that the more civil, supportive, and interpersonally sensitive elements of women's style will not be lost.

REFERENCES

Abramson, Lyn Y., Martin E. P. Seligman, and John D. Teasdale. 1978. Learned Helplessness in Humans: Critique and Reformulation. *Journal of Abnormal Psychology* 87:49–74.

Anderson, Bruce. 1996. Culture, Subculture, and Microculture. In *Exploring Social Issues,* edited by Dana Dunn, William Stacey, and Frank Weed. Englewood Cliffs, N.J.: Prentice-Hall.

Argyle, Michael. 1994. *The Psychology of Social Class.* New York: Routledge.

Aries, Elizabeth. 1976. Interaction Patterns and Themes of Male, Female, and Mixed Groups. *Small Group Behavior* 7:1.7–18.

———. 1987. Gender and Communication. In *Sex and Gender,* edited by Phillip Shaver and Clyde Hendrick. Newbury Park, Calif.: Sage.

Axtell, Roger E. 1991. *Gestures.* New York: Wiley.

Barreca, Regina, ed. 1996. *The Penguin Book of Women's Humor.* New York: Penguin.

Bate, Barbara. 1988. *Communication and the Sexes.* New York: Harper and Row.

Beck, Aaron T., A. John Rush, Brian F. Shaw, and Gary Emery. 1979. *Cognitive Therapy of Depression.* New York: Guilford.

Bend, Ruth. 1975. Male–Female Intonation Patterns in American English. In *Language and Sex: Difference and Dominance,* edited by Barrie Thorne and Nancy Henley. Rowley, Mass.: Newbury House.

Berger, Charles R. 1979. Beyond Initial Interaction: Uncertainty, Understanding, and the Development of Interpersonal Relationships. In *Language and Social Psychology,* edited by Howard Giles and Robert N. St. Clair. Baltimore: University Park Press.

Beschloss, Michael R. 1991. *The Crisis Years: Kennedy and Khrushchev, 1960–1963.* New York: Edward Burlingame.

Birdwhistell, Ray L. 1970. *Kinesics and Context.* Philadelphia: University of Pennsylvania Press.

Blum, Ronald. 1995. LA's Nomo Named Top NL Rookie. *Dallas Morning News,* November 10.

Bohn, Emil, and Randall Stutman. 1983. Sex-Role Differences in the Relational Control Dimension of Dyadic Interaction. *Women's Studies in Communication* 6:96–104.

Brislin, Richard, Kenneth Cushner, Craig Cherrie, and Mahealani Yong. 1986. *Intercultural Interactions: A Practical Guide.* Beverly Hills: Sage.

Brody, Mitchell D. 1980. *Get Some Respect.* New York: Holt, Rinehart and Winston.

Brown, Roger. 1965. *Social Psychology.* New York: Free Press.

Bruner, Jerome S., and L. Postman. 1949. Perception, Cognition, and Behavior. *Journal of Personality* 18:14–31.

Buss, Arnold H. 1980. *Self-Consciousness and Social Anxiety*. San Francisco: W. H. Freeman.

Cameron, Deborah, Fiona McAlinden, and Kathy O'Leary. 1988. Lakoff in Context: The Social and Linguistic Functions of Tag Questions. In *Women in Their Speech Communities*, edited by Jennifer Coates and Deborah Cameron. New York: Longman.

Cantor, Joanne R. 1976. What is Funny to Whom? The Role of Gender. *Journal of Communication* 26:164–172.

Carroll, Raymonde. 1988. *Cultural Misunderstandings*. Translated by Carol Volk. Chicago: University of Chicago Press.

Coates, Jennifer. 1986. *Women, Men and Language*. New York: Longman.

Condry, John, and Sandra Condry. 1976. Sex Differences: A Study of the Eye of the Beholder. *Child Development* 47:812–819.

Cooley, Charles H. 1902. *Human Nature and the Social Order*. New York: Scribner's.

Crawford, Mary. 1995. *Talking Difference*. London: Sage.

Crawford, Mary, and Diane Gressley. 1991. Creativity, Caring, and Context: Women's and Men's Accounts of Humor Preferences and Practices. *Psychology of Women Quarterly* 15:217–231.

David, Deborah S., and Robert Brannon. 1976. *The Forty-Nine Percent Majority: The Male Sex Role*. Reading, Mass.: Addison-Wesley.

Davis, James Allan, and Tom W. Smith. 1991. *General Social Surveys, 1972–1991*. Machine-readable data file. Storrs: Roper Center for Public Opinion Research, University of Connecticut.

Duncan, Starkey. 1972. Some Signals and Rules for Taking Speaking Turns in Conversations. *Journal of Personality and Social Psychology* 23(2):283–292.

Dutton, D. G., and A. P. Aron. 1974. Some Evidence for Heightened Sexual Attraction under Conditions of High Anxiety. *Journal of Personality and Social Psychology* 30:510–517.

Eder, Donna, with Catherine Colleen Evans and Steven Parker. 1995. *School Talk*. New Brunswick, N.J.: Rutgers University Press.

Eder, Donna, and Maureen T. Hallinan. 1978. Sex Differences in Children's Friendships. *American Sociological Review* 43:237–250.

Edwards, Gavin. 1995. *'Scuse Me While I Kiss This Guy*. Illustrated by Chris Kalib. New York: Fireside.

Ellul, Jacques. 1965. *Propaganda: The Formation of Men's Attitudes*. New York: Knopf.

Flavell, John H., with Patricia T. Botkin, Charles L. Fry, Jr., John W. Wright, and Paul E. Jarvis. 1968. *The Development of Role-Taking and Communication Skills in Children*. New York: Wiley.

Frank, Mark G., and Thomas Gilovich. 1988. The Dark Side of Self and Social Perception: Black Uniforms and Aggression in Professional Sports. *Journal of Personality and Social Psychology* 54:74–85.

Freud, S. 1965. *The Psychopathology of Everyday Life*. Translated and edited by J. Strachey. New York: Norton.

Furnham, A. 1990. Language and Personality. In *Handbook of Language and Social Psychology,* edited by H. Giles and P. Robinson. Chichester, England: Wiley.

Fussell, Paul. 1983. *Class.* New York: Ballantine.

Gamson, William A. 1968. *Power and Discontent.* Homewood, Ill.: Dorsey Press.

Garfinkel, Harold. 1967. *Studies in Ethnomethodology.* Englewood Cliffs, N.J.: Prentice-Hall.

Goffman, Erving. 1956. Embarrassment and Social Organization. *American Journal of Sociology* 62:264–274.

Goldberg, Philip. 1975. Are Women Prejudiced against Women? In *Psychology Is Social,* edited by Edward Krupat. Glenview, Ill.: Scott, Foresman.

Graham, John L., and Yoshihiro Sano. 1984. *Smart Bargaining: Doing Business with the Japanese.* Cambridge, Mass.: Ballinger.

Gray, John. 1992. *Men Are from Mars, Women Are from Venus.* New York: Harper Collins.

Grimes, Michael D., and Joan M. Morris. 1997. *Caught in the Middle: Contradictions in the Lives of Sociologists from Working-Class Backgrounds.* Westport, Conn.: Praeger.

Hall, Edward T. 1966. *The Hidden Dimension.* New York: Doubleday.

Hall, Edward T., and Mildred Reed Hall. 1987. *Hidden Differences.* Garden City, N.Y.: Anchor Press/Doubleday.

Hoffer, Bates, and Richard G. Santos. 1977. Cultural Clashes in Kinesics. In *Aspects of Nonverbal Communication,* edited by Walburga von Raffler-Engle and Bates Hoffer. San Antonio: Trinity University Press.

Hoijer, Harry. 1964. Cultural Implications of Some Navajo Linguistic Categories. In *Language in Culture and Society,* edited by Dell Hymes. New York: Harper and Row.

Holt, Grace Sims. 1972. Inversion in Black Communication. In *Rappin' and Stylin' Out,* edited by Thomas Kochman. Urbana: University of Illinois Press.

Illich, Ivan. 1970. *Celebration of Awareness.* Garden City, N.Y.: Doubleday.

Keirsey, David, and Marilyn Bates. 1984. *Please Understand Me: Character and Temperament Types.* Del Mar, Calif.: Prometheus Nemesis.

Kinch, John W. 1973. *Social Psychology.* New York: McGraw-Hill.

Kochman, Thomas. 1981. *Black and White Styles in Conflict.* Chicago: University of Chicago Press.

Labov, William. 1972. Rules for Ritual Insults. In *Rappin' and Stylin' Out,* edited by Thomas Kochman. Urbana: University of Illinois Press.

LaFrance, Marianne, and Clara Mayo. 1976. Racial Differences in Gaze Behavior during Conversations: Two Systematic Observational Studies. *Journal of Personality and Social Psychology* 33(5):547–552.

Lakoff, Robin. 1975. *Language and Woman's Place.* New York: Harper Colophone.

———. 1990. *Talking Power.* New York: Basic Books.

Lehtonen, Jaakko, and Keri Sajavaara. 1985. The Silent Finn. In *Perspectives on Silence,* edited by Deborah Tannen and Muriel Saville-Troike. Norwood, N.J.: Ablex.

Lever, Janet. 1978. Sex Differences in the Complexity of Children's Play and Games. *American Sociological Review* 43:471–483.

Maltz, Daniel N., and Ruth A. Borker. 1982. A Cultural Approach to Male–Female Miscommunication. In *Language and Social Identity*, edited by John J. Gumperz. Cambridge: Cambridge University Press.

Mead, George H. 1934. *Mind, Self, and Society*. Chicago: University of Chicago Press.

Mehrabian, Albert. 1981. *Silent Messages*. Belmont, Calif.: Wadsworth.

Merton, Robert K. 1949. *Social Theory and Social Structure*. Glencoe, Ill.: Free Press.

Miller, Peggy. 1986. Teasing as Language Socialization and Verbal Play in a White Working-Class Community. In *Language Socialization Across Cultures*, edited by Bambi B. Schieffelin and Elinor Ochs. Cambridge: Cambridge University Press.

Mills, C. Wright. 1940. Situated Actions and Vocabularies of Motives. *American Sociological Review* 5:904–913.

Mishra, Arpita. 1982. Discovering Connections. In *Language and Social Identity*, edited by John J. Gumperz. Cambridge: Cambridge University Press.

Mitchell-Kernan, Claudia. 1972. Signifying, Loud-Talking and Marking. In *Rappin' and Stylin' Out*, edited by Thomas Kochman. Urbana: University of Illinois Press.

Modigliani, Andre. 1968. Embarrassment and Embarrassability. *Sociometry* 31:331–326.

Nathanson, Donald L. 1992. *Shame and Pride*. New York: Norton.

Neisser, Ulric. 1976. *Cognition and Reality*. San Francisco: W. H. Freeman.

Patterson, Christopher, Amy Semmel, Carl von Baeyer, Lyn Y. Abramson, Gerald I. Metalsky, and Martin E. P. Seligman. 1982. The Attributional Style Questionnaire. *Cognitive Therapy and Research* 6:287–300.

Penfield, Joyce. 1989. Social and Linguistic Parameters of Prosody in Chicano English. In *English across Cultures: Cultures across English*, edited by Ofelia Garcia and Ricardo Otheguy. New York: Mouton de Gruyter.

Petras, Ross, and Kathryn Petras. 1993. *The 776 Stupidest Things Ever Said*. New York: Main Street Books.

Pettigrew, Thomas F. 1979. The Ultimate Attribution Error: Extending Allport's Cognitive Analysis of Prejudice. *Personality and Social Psychology Bulletin* 5:461–476.

Powers, William T. 1973. *Behavior: The Control of Perception*. Chicago: Aldine.

Rosenthal, Robert, and Lenore Jacobson. 1968. *Pygmalion in the Classroom: Teacher Expectation and Pupils' Intellectual Development*. New York: Holt, Rinehart and Winston.

Ross, Lee D., Teresa M. Amabile, and Julia L. Steinmetz. 1977. Social Roles, Social Control, and Biases in Social-Perception Processes. *Journal of Personality and Social Psychology* 35:485–494.

Rowland, D. 1993. *Japanese Business Etiquette*. New York: Warner.

Rubin, Jeffrey Z., Frank J. Provenzano, and Zella Luria. 1974. The Eye of the Beholder: Parents' Views on Sex of Newborns. *American Journal of Orthopsychiatry* 44:512–519.

Saunders, George R. 1985. Silence and Noise as Emotion Management Styles: An Italian Case. In *Perspectives on Silence,* edited by Deborah Tannen and Muriel Saville-Troike. Norwood, N.J.: Ablex.

Saville-Troike, Muriel. 1985. The Place of Silence in an Integrated Theory of Communication. In *Perspectives on Silence,* edited by Deborah Tannen and Muriel Saville-Troike. Norwood, N.J.: Ablex.

Schachter, S. 1964. The Interaction of Cognitive and Physiological Determinants of Emotional State. In *Advances in Experimental Social Psychology,* edited by L. Berkowitz. Vol. 1. New York: Academic Press.

Schaufeli, W. B. 1988. Perceiving the Causes of Unemployment: An Evaluation of the Causal Dimensions Scale in a Real-Life Situation. *Journal of Personality and Social Psychology* 54:347–356.

Schutz, Alfred. 1971. *Collected Papers I: The Problem of Social Reality.* The Hague: Martinus Nijhoff.

Sennett, Richard, and Jonathan Cobb. 1972. *The Hidden Injuries of Class.* New York: Norton.

Sheldon, Amy. 1993. Pickle Fights: Gendered Talk in Preschool Disputes. In *Gender and Conversational Interaction,* edited by Deborah Tannen. New York: Oxford University Press.

Snyder, Mark. 1974. Self-Monitoring of Expressive Behavior. *Journal of Personality and Social Psychology* 30:526–537.

Sperber, Dan, and D. Wilson. 1981. Irony and the Use–Mention Distinction. In *Radical Pragmatics,* edited by P. Cole. New York: Academic Press.

Steele, Shelby. 1988. *The Content of Our Character.* New York: St. Martin's.

Sweeney, Paul D., Karen Anderson, and Scott Bailey. 1986. Attributional Style in Depression: A Meta-Analytic Review. *Journal of Personality and Social Psychology* 50:974–991.

Tannen, Deborah. 1985. Silence: Anything But. In *Perspectives on Silence,* edited by Deborah Tannen and Muriel Saville-Troike. Norwood, N.J.: Ablex.

———. 1990. *You Just Don't Understand.* New York: Ballantine.

———. 1994. *Talking from 9 to 5.* New York: William Morrow.

———. 1996. *Gender and Discourse.* New York: Oxford University Press

Universal Pictures. 1945. *The Naughty Nineties.* A motion picture starring Bud Abbott and Lou Costello.

Vargas, Marjorie Fink. 1986. *Louder Than Words.* Ames: University of Iowa Press.

Vogel, Dena Ann, Margaret A. Lake, Susan Evans, and Katherine Hildebrandt Karrader. 1991. Children's and Adults' Sex-Stereotype Perceptions of Infants. *Sex Roles* 24:605–616.

Walker, Anne Griffam. 1985. The Two Faces of Silence: The Effect of Witness Hesitancy on Lawyers' Impressions. In *Perspectives on Silence,* edited by Deborah Tannen and Muriel Saville-Troike. Norwood, N.J.: Ablex.

White, Joseph L., and Thomas A. Parham. 1990. *The Psychology of Blacks.* 2d ed. Englewood Cliffs, N.J.: Prentice-Hall.

Williams, Annette Powell. 1972. Dynamics of a Black Audience. In *Rappin' and Stylin' Out,* edited by Thomas Kochman. Urbana: University of Illinois Press.

Young, Linda Wai Ling. 1982. Inscrutability Revisited. In *Language and Social Identity,* edited by John J. Gumperz. Cambridge: Cambridge University Press.

Young, Robert L. 1991. Race, Conceptions of Crime and Justice, and Support for the Death Penalty. *Social Psychology Quarterly* 54:67–75.

———. 1995a. Intentions, Interpretations, and Misunderstandings. *Sociological Spectrum* 15:161–180.

———. 1995b. Misunderstandings as Accounts. *Sociological Inquiry* 66:251–264.

Zborowski, Mark. 1953. Cultural Components in Responses to Pain. *The Journal of Social Issues* 8:16–31.

Zimmerman, Don, and Candice West. 1975. Sex roles, interruptions and silences in conversation. In *Language and Sex: Difference and Dominance,* edited by Barrie Thorne and Nancy Henley. Rowley, Mass.: Newbury House.

INDEX